BIPOLAR DISORDER

Learn the Symptoms and Strategies on How You Can Cope

(The Complete Bipolar Disorder Survival Guide to Stopping Mood Swings)

Mildred Sanders

Published By Ryan Princeton

Mildred Sanders

All Rights Reserved

Bipolar Disorder: Learn the Symptoms and Strategies on How You Can Cope (The Complete Bipolar Disorder Survival Guide to Stopping Mood Swings)

ISBN 978-1-77485-271-2

Legal & Disclaimer

The information contained in this book is not designed to replace or take the place of any form of medicine or professional medical advice. The information in this book has been provided for educational and entertainment purposes only.

The information contained in this book has been compiled from sources deemed reliable, and it is accurate to the best of the Author's knowledge; however, the Author cannot guarantee its accuracy and validity and cannot be held liable for any errors or omissions. Changes are periodically made to this book. You must consult your doctor or get professional medical advice before using any of the suggested remedies, techniques, or information in this book.

TABLE OF CONTENTS

Introduction

The life of a person with bipolar disorder isn't an easy task. One day, you experience euphoria. You believe that you are able to dominate the world. You believe that you are able to achieve everything. Then, the next day, you are overwhelmed with sadness. You feel helpless and insignificant. You're afraid to die.

Bipolar disorder can make you feel depressed. It may hinder people from having healthy relationships. It may prevent you from reaching all the potential that you can.

Today, more than 30 million people across the globe are affected by bipolar disorders, and it's the sixth most frequent cause of the inability of a person to live a an ordinary life. Bipolar disorder can cause havoc to career and relationships. The following are the ways this disorder can wreck havoc on your life:

It hinders your ability earn money.

1

It can cause you to make bad life choices.

It is difficult to build solid and long-lasting relationships.

It causes auditory and visual hallucinations.

It makes you feel that your life is out of balance.

It could affect your work and social function.

It increases your risk to a variety of medical issues like thyroid disorders, migraines, chronic pain, heart disease and obesity. It can also increase your risk of developing diabetes.

It can cause suicide. Research shows that one out of five bipolar patients successfully commit suicide.

It can destroy your life.

The bipolar disorder is like fighting in the brain. You know that something is wrong.

However, in your heart you're not worried. Therefore, anything could happen.

Bipolar disorder was kind of taboo for a long time. Now the disease is being widely talked about and many who suffer from this illness are seeking help.

The book provides important information to aid you in understanding bipolar disorder. The book also offers guidelines and tips on managing bipolar symptoms and how to live successfully with bipolar disorder.

If you're struggling with bipolar disorder, you'll think that your life isn't progressing. It's easy to feel stuck. However, there's a way out. In reality, there are many people suffering from bipolar disorder that are enjoying their careers as well as relationships and life generally. Numerous actors, lawyers, politicians and singers, as well as artists and journalists have been able to achieve success in their careers despite having bipolar disorder. There are many famous names such as Patrick

Kennedy, Jane Pauley, Catherine Zeta-Jones, Russell Brand, Demi Lovato, Patrick Kennedy, Jean-Claude Van Damme, Chris Brown, Stephen Fry, Axl Rose, and Frank Bruno have all struggled with bipolar disorder.

Chapter 1: What is Bipolar Disorder?

The disease was initially identified and initially defined as manic depressive disease in the work of Emil Kraepelin. It's a term used to describe a state that is characterised by periods of high mood, characterised by a lack of happiness, excessive energy, anger, and a reduction of sleep, and decisions that are not thought through and without thought of the consequences as well as periods of depression when the patient is not in contact with other people or has a negative outlook on life, and occasionally outbursts of crying.

BPD is associated with a rate of more than 6% suicides in the span of 20 years after the first symptoms and 30-to-40% incidence of self-inflicted injuries. This is increased by any type of drug abuse, and also if you are suffering from BPD there is any type of anxiety disorder is present.

The cause of the disorder isn't fully comprehended and explained by scientists. But, the contributing factors have been identified. These are the factors:

Genetic

A moderate to mild effect can be induced on BPD by chromosomal areas and genes that have a tendency to susceptibility. The likelihood of the onset of the disease in the first degree relatives of the patient is 10 times greater than the likelihood of it surfacing on the average population.

Physiological

MRIs have revealed that there are a variety of structural defects in particular brain circuits, which could be associated with functional abnormalities. There is a reason to believe that that these irregularities could be the cause behind the disorder , however this can been proven as at this time.

Environmental

There is plenty of evidence to suggest that a variety of environmental factors contribute significantly to the development of BPD. The facets that can contribute to BPD include:

Recent major events and dramatic changes in relationships and life

Childhood abuse and trauma

Harsh family atmosphere

Work-related issues

Neurological

The most common cause is the presence of a neurological disease such as stroke HIV infections, porphyria or brain injury caused by multiple sclerosis and trauma.

Neuro-endocrinological

Dopamine, that is a neurotransmitter associated with mood swings together with gamma-Aminobutyric acids (otherwise called GABA) as well as glutamate dramatically increase the probability of having mood swings that are elevated.

The neuro-endocrinological factors is the main reason for the need for a correct diagnosis. In other conditions, like the panic disorder, gaba can be an acknowledged beneficiary agent, but in bipolar disorder, it can be quite dangerous.

Evolutionary

Theory of Evolution suggests that the genes that cause BPD could have been eliminated by nature. But the reality that there are many BPD sufferers around the world suggests that these genes are receiving an evolutionary benefit.

Bipolar disorder isn't one disorder. It's a spectrum of four distinct conditions:

1) Bipolar I

In order for the disorder to qualify as bipolar, it needs to be at minimum one condition that is characterized by elevated mood. This makes the diagnosis. Although depression-related states are common however, they're not required to diagnose,

2)Bipolar II

Bipolar II's characteristics include at the very least one hypomanic episode, and several major phases of depression. The hypomanic event is less severe than a manic attack (which is also described as an elevated state) and is not associated with psychosis or impairment in occupational or social relationships.

3)Cyclothymia

This is among the most common problems faced by close people who are near with the sufferer. In general, it is viewed as a trait of personality and is viewed as a negative. It is characterized by a series of low-intensity hypomanic and depression episodes that cause problems with normal activities.

4.) NOS (which stands for not otherwise specifically)

Anything that does not be classified as one of the previously mentioned disorders is considered to be a part of this group. The primary aspect is that the manic-hypermanic cycle depression, and hypomanic episodes impedes and alters to varying levels the daily life that the person suffers.

The majority of patients who meet the criteria of those on the BPD spectrum, suffer from 0.4 up to 0.7 episodes each year with the duration of each episode between three and six months. Most of the time, there is a remission time between episodes that lasts approximately two months. The rate at which the interval between moods is the main determinant for the course of disorder.

The conventional medical approaches for treating BPD include psychotherapy as well as medication that are mood stabilizers, such as lithium and anticonvulsants, as well as antipsychotic compounds like benzodiazepines. If patients are not responding to other treatments, electroconvulsive therapy could be beneficial.

A brief overview and treatment options for bipolar disorder show how serious the condition is. But with the help of simple daily tasks to take care of, it could be managed and overcome to allow the sufferer to lead a normal life.

Chapter 2: What You Can Do to build support for your relationships.

It doesn't matter the field you work working in or what role you're in, knowing how to build compatibility will give you a lot of chances. In the end, if you are able to connect with someone, the person you are attempting to connect with is likely to be able to assist you in success.

Some people might argue that it's the benefits of having a character It is possible to build a bond with individuals , or not. But this isn't the whole story. The degree of affinity can increase over time however, anyone can maintain and enhance compatibility, in the same way as other skills.

What is affinity? and how can you become adept in making affinity? We'll explore this, and more here in the article.

What is Rapport?

Compatibility is the basis for essential, close and friendly relationships between people. It's the feeling of belonging that you experience when you meet someone you trust and admire and from whose viewpoint you can relate to. The bonds are formed when you realize that you have in common traits and desires throughout the course of your life.

According to researchers Linda Tickle-Degnen and Robert Rosenthal, when you are compatible with someone who shares:

Shared mindfulness means that you're equally focused on the topic and are interested in what the other person is saying or doing.

Inspiration: You're neighbors and happy and that you think of each other.

Coordination: you are "in the state of harmony" in your relationship and have an average understanding. Your levels of vitality as well as tone and non-verbal communication also are identical.

This connection may manifest in a flash - once the two of you "click" with someone - or develop slowly, over certain period of time. It could develop naturally with no planning, or you could decide to create it.

Affinity isn't just an instrument to build connections, however it's also the basis of advancement. If you're able to connect with someone, you're better placed to influence, educate and teach, particularly due to the fact that you've come up with methods others are likely to be open to your ideas, to communicate information, and open up opportunities.

Whatever the reason, whether you're targeted for a profession selling something or trying to enhance relationships, knowing how to create compatibility will help you to perform effectively.

Tip:

Affinity is similar to trust. It is possible to create trust and affinity simultaneously however, compatibility focuses more on establishing an association or security, however trust is more dependent on establishing a reputation for unflagging quality, consistency and being faithful to your promises.

Instructions to Create Rapport

Compatibility is a two-way connection between two people, which means it's not something you can separate from others. In all cases, discover ways to improve your relationship by taking these steps.

Beware:

Use your judgment when employing these strategies. Don't use them in a way that is unwise or unscrupulous to offer people something they would not normally require, for example, or to manipulate them into a strategy which is not in their best interest or advantages.

1. Be Sure to Check Your Appearance

The first introductions you make and your attire should aid in connecting with people, and not be an obstacle. The best general rule of thumb is to dress slightly "better" than the people who you'll be meeting. However should you arrive and discover that you're wearing a dress that's too big then you'll be able to change your clothes to fit the occasion.

2. Remember the basics

Recollect all nuts and bolts in good correspondence :

You should be socially compatible .

Grin.

Unwind .

Remember people's names .

Keep your head straight and maintain a steady posture.

Pay attention carefully and with a keen eye .

Be careful not to extend your time.

These fundamental principles guide the development of remarkable correspondence. It is difficult to create a sense of compatibility without them. They can help you build trust, empathy and a inclination to people you're paying attention to.

3. Find Common Ground

Sharing a common opinion will build trust and trust, so make use of casual chat to find something you and your partner have in common.

A majority of people enjoy talking about themselves. The more genuine you are in the group, the more likely they will loosen to "open to the world." Make use of open-ended inquiries to uncover specific information: perhaps you attended the same school, have the same hobbies, spent your the same childhood in a city, or join a similar group of gamers. Even just sharing your displeasure with the traffic that delayed your work-related activities can help you to get closer to someone.

Tip 1.

It's important to be honest and honest and refrain from exaggerating things. Don't create an interest or even make an effort just to show a sense of affinity. This is not only an appearance of being unsettling and arousing, but it could also undermine your credibility!

Tip 2.

It is an amazing method to build trust, but make sure to use humor with caution. It is not possible for everyone to make a joke however, what might appear like a good joke to you may be offensive to an individual. If you think there's a chance that your comment could be misinterpreted, do not make the mistake of remarking.

4. Create Shared Experiences

The development of affinity is not possible without human connection The most effective way to work together is to create new, mutually beneficial encounters.

These encounters can be as simple as attending a similar gathering or as complicated as co-coordinating a board process. Collaborating to identify problems, create strategies, and organize procedures, for example it can help make you and the other individuals closer.

You can be familiar with other 210 skills in the field like this through joining Mind Tools Club. Mind Tools Club.

5. Be compassionate

Sympathy is a way of being able to understand other people by looking at things from their perspective and observing their emotions. To comprehend and appreciate the viewpoint of someone else it is essential to understand the most important thing to him. As we've already mentioned many people enjoy discussing their opinions, preferences, and wants, as well as issues and triumphs, so make sure you inquire openly and give the opportunity to speak.

It is essential to listen carefully the words of others, so that you are able to respond with curiosity. This is why you must be a good listener and also to refine your passion perception . It is also possible to use perceptual Positions which are a technique for looking at things from different people perspectives.

Tip:

It's difficult to develop an emotional connection with someone who has to talk only about herself. Therefore, try to change the topic. Try to be as open as the other person does. You'll feel more and more happy as a result.

6. Mirror and Match

Studies show that we tend towards people who appear as being similar as us. Reflecting and coordinating are ways for building compatibility , by becoming more similar to the other person.

The way you express this is not about what you say. A psychologist named Albert

Mehrabian found that the words we use to communicate represent just seven percent of the correspondence we have regarding our feelings or states of mind. The concept of voice is the largest percentage (38 percent) as well as our non-verbal communication accounts for more than 55 percent. In this way, you'll experience the loss of a performance when you do not take into account your "entire image" of human interaction.

In this regard, try these steps to create compatibility:

Be aware of the other person's nonverbal communications, which include gestures, stances and articulations. If such as, for example, the person is laying his jaw on the left side of his hand, think about mirroring him using your right hand. To match it you could use the left side of your hand.

Receive a comparative personality. If the other person is outgoing or thoughtful excessive, brash or apathetic and awe-inspiring, you should continue in the same manner. If you've saved him, for instance then you must be also, otherwise, you'll end up being seen as uninformed or inconsiderate.

Utilize comparable language . If he uses straightforward, simple words, then you shouldalso. If you speak in a specific language and you are able to you should match his style. It is also possible to repeat key or the most popular phrases or words.

Be in sync with the other's conversation patterns, for instance, beat, tone and volume. For instance If you notice that he speaks softly and slowly you can then turn the volume and the beat in your vocal. (Research conducted by the U.S. Government Bureau of Investigation recommends this as the most effective method of setting an friendship. It's subtle, yet it makes the person you're talking to feel at ease and feel like they're being understood.)

Good judgment and care are essential when coordinating and reflecting. For instance, don't impersonate every word or sign. If you do, you risk creating an offense. Keep your appearance hidden and try to reach a point that you're usually conducting your behavior in a coordinated manner in order to ensure that the person in front of you is unaware of the actions you're taking.

Reflecting and coordinating are difficult to master. In any case be aware that we all do not realize that we mirror and match family members or friends and partners every day. If you have to practice try using the technique of pretending .

Tip:

If you consider non-verbal communication as a way to communicate They'll see that you're thinking and that could result in a opposite effect to the one that you require. In this regard do not be unthinking. Be loose and comfortable.

Restoring Rapport

It is a significant investment to alter affinity after it is lost.

First, you must address why you did not feel as if you had a connection in any event. Be honest and clear and what exactly transpired. If you are required to apologize , treat it the right thing by apologizing.

Then, you must think of ways to repair any damaged trust. Do more effort in the event that you need to maintain your wording. Sincerity and genuine concern about the needs of another person can be a significant factor in reestablishing trust and rebuilding compatibility.

Key Tips

You build compatibility when you establish trust, connection and a sense of pity for someone.

Affinity building can be incredibly helpful to your professional career This can help you establish strong relationships and will open up many doors for you.

Follow these six steps to create compatibility:

Make sure you are in good shape.

Remember that nuts and bolts are the basis that are of good correspondence.

Find common conviction.

Have a shared experience.

Be compassionate.

Mirror and match idiosyncrasies , and talk in a way that is appropriate. It is best to work on compatibility for a long time. But, you could use these methods to build quickly, in case you need to.

So, you can try these methods to make similarity:

Be aware of the other person's nonverbal conversation, which includes gesture, posture, and verbalization. For instance, if you notice that he is placing the left side of his mouth on top, consider mirroring him using your left hand. To organize it using the hand you have left.

Choose a friend. If the other person is warm or friendly or even a bit shy and apprehensive, you must follow in the same way. If he's not spared for instance, then you must be too, or risk being considered unwise or a celebrity.

Use similar language . If he is using explicit, concise phrases, then you must, too. If he teaches in a specific language, then help him to use the style. It is also possible to recite the most popular phrases or words.

Be in tune with the talk of the other plans For instance, beat, tone and volume. For instance, if the person talks softly and steps through each step, you can reduce in volume as well as beat. (Research conducted by the U.S. Government Bureau of Investigation suggests this is the most effective way to establish a relationship that is likable. It's subtle and yet helps the other person feel more secure and feel like they're getting noticed.)

The importance of trust and watchfulness is paramount when it comes to organizing and reflecting. Do not, for instance, imitate every word or sign. When you do this, you could end up creating offence. Make sure you are subtle and plan to arrive at a spot that you're usually making your voice sound synchronized in the hope that the person you're addressing is unaware of the actions you're taking.

Reflecting and organizing are difficult for experts. It is important to remember that we all often mirror and compare with our family, friends and colleagues each day. If you are required to work on it, you can try your imagination to imagine .

Tip:

If people look at non-verbal communications it will be apparent the impression that you're reflecting. This might have a negative result to what you want. Therefore, don't be naive Be open and empathetic.

Reestablishing Rapport

It takes a certain amount of effort to change proclivity after it is lost.

In any event, explain the reason why you didn't like yourself. Be honest and clear about and briefly what transpired. If you have to apologize , do so in the same manner.

Then, look at strategies to repair any trust that has been damaged. Do extra effort if necessary and ensure that you have kept your announcement. Being straightforward and genuinely concerned to meet the needs of the other will help in establishing trust and reestablishing a sense of commonality.

Key Aspects

You will collect similarity when establish trust, friendship and attraction to an individual.

Building a sense of partiality can be incredibly beneficial to your career This is why it's important to create amazing social groups, and this could open up a variety of possibilities for you.

Try to follow these six phases for the following similarities:

Make sure you are looking presentable.

Keep at the top of your prioritized list of the scattered pieces of correspondence that are good.

*Discover shared convictions.

*Share experiences.

Feel empathy.

Mirror and match particularities and converse in a manner that is appropriate. It is best to work on similarity with time. However, you can apply these concepts to build the concept quickly, if require it.

Chapter 3: The Myths and facts on Bipolar Disorder

The people who aren't as sensitive or knowledgeable about bipolar disorder could be deluded and believe in common misconceptions regarding bipolar disorder. They are merely demonstrating that they are ignorant of bipolar disorder and are not the people you should consult in order to determine whether you suffer from bipolar disorder. that you suffer from.

Here are some myths and truths about bipolar disorder that circulate all over the internet today.

The myth: "People with bipolar disorder are insane, and always swing between of depression and manic episodes."

The fact is that the majority of people who suffer from bipolar disorder are much more depressed than people who are manic.

In the event that manic-like episodes happen it could be small and go unnoticed.

A majority of people can go for long durations (days months, days and more.) without ever showing any signs or having any symptoms.

The Myth "Bipolar illness is not manageable without treatment. Treatment is the only hope that will keep the bipolar disorders under your control."

The truth is that even though medication is among the most effective treatments for bipolar disorder , there are many other options for treating the condition and aid you in managing your symptoms more effectively.

A balanced diet, plenty of sleep, regular exercise therapies, and self-help strategies will assist you in managing issues better and could even help you beat the bipolar disorder that you suffer from.

Myths: "You will not be in a position to lead a healthy and normal life when you have bipolar disorder."

Truth: People who suffer from bipolar disorder tend to have excellent jobs, healthy relationships and happy families.

Although the bipolar disorder that you suffer from is a lot of issues, it's crucial to be aware that you can conquer the challenges without fear and trusting in your support system whenever you require.

Myths "Bipolar disorders only have an impact upon how you feel."

The truth:

While there are some tests available at home Bipolar disorder is largely genetic.

This test is the only one that will determine if your genes place you at a greater likelihood of developing or developing bipolar disorder.

The best method to find out if you are suffering from bipolar disorder is to speak with your physician. The doctor is in a position to help you identify the problem and assist you in identifying, and perhaps debunking the symptoms you suspect.

The Myth "There exists a method to test to determine whether you suffer from bipolar disorder. Therefore, you must take the time to be tested.

Truth: Many people believe of bipolar disorders as merely about mood swings that are constant, depression, and a few instances of depression. But, it affects your mood and mood, memory, concentration confidence, energy levels and appetite. Bipolar disorder is able to trigger a range of health problems , such as the high pressure of blood, coronary disease anxiety, diabetes and migraines.

Myth:

"Bipolar disorder is an invented condition. It's not actually a real thing."

The truth:

Bipolar disorder is a disease. People who take it casually are unaware that it is treatable and that recovery is a long-term process that requires effort and time as well as honest effort. Bipolar disorder shouldn't be viewed as something to be overlooked, as when left untreated, people may be injured mentally, physically or and mentally or even all three.

Myth:

"Children do not have bipolar. This is impossible!

The truth:

The symptoms of bipolar disorder may affect children as young as 6 years old. Children who suffer from bipolar disorder are more likely to have parents with the disorder, and may experience intense mood swings or transitions between depression and mania.

Myth:

"You will be dependent on the bipolar medications and won't be as clean as you ought to be."

The truth:

Although it is possible to develop dependence to medications, it'll be very difficult to do so when you use the medication according to what is recommended. The medication is intended to help you manage your mood. If you decide to use drugs in order to manage bipolar disorder it is best to take the medication according to the directions.

Myth:

"Therapy isn't working. There's nothing to it but crying and moaning. What can you do to aid you in dealing with such a serious disorder as bipolar disorder?"

Truth:

Therapy has been evaluated and has been proven to be an efficient method of treating bipolar disorder. The benefits of talking to others are immense. Talk therapy can assist you to discover the triggers that are causing your behavior, and assist you in taking appropriate steps to manage yourself.

Myth:

"Treatment are for those who are inactive and weak to handle their issues by themselves."

The truth:

The process of seeking treatment is a major decision that requires a huge amount of confidence.

There is no weakness in you If you choose seeking treatment. You will only strengthen yourself by recognizing that you suffer from bipolar disorder and stepping beyond yourself to seek assistance. The treatment you seek and the advice of others can be helpful to those who feel as or have bipolar disorder.

Chapter 4: Medicines To Treat Bipolar Disorder

Medicine is the mainstay of a proper bipolar disorder treatment program. Different medications can help control manic and depressive symptoms. However, these medications could cause dangerous side effects, so it is important to take these drugs with care.

How to Increase The Effect of the medication

Here are some suggestions to enable you to get the most benefit from your medications:

1.Use natural mood stabilizers.

Your lifestyle could influence the symptoms you experience. If you live a healthy and balanced lifestyle then you'll require less medication. Therefore, it's crucial to make use of natural mood stabilizers, such as nutritious foods and exercises.

2.Avoid the use of anti-depressants.

It is important to keep in mind that bipolar depression differs from the normal clinical depression. Antidepressants taken during depressive episodes may trigger hypomanic or manic symptoms. Therefore, take antidepressants with care. It is best to test the mood stabilizers initially.

3.Try therapy.

Keep in mind that taking medication on its own is not enough. You must seek therapy. Therapy will provide you with the tools needed to assist you in overcoming the challenges of life. One-on-one sessions with your therapist will aid in monitoring your improvement. Therapy can also assist you to deal with or treat the bipolar symptoms that are adversely affect your work and personal life.

4.Continue to take your mood stabilizers as well as bipolar medication even if you are feeling better.

You must adhere to the prescriptions of your physician. Therefore, you must take your medications even if you're not having symptoms or you are generally feeling more relaxed.

Making the Right Choice for the right medication

Keep in mind that different patients react differently to different bipolar medications. Therefore, in order to select the appropriate medication, you must undergo the "trial and trial and" procedure. It may take a long time until you have found the ideal dosage and medication. Therefore, take your time However, if your medication makes you feel sick, talk about this with your physician right now.

Before you begin the new medication you are taking to treat your illness, you'll need to ask yourself these questions:

Do I take any other medications that may interfere the mood stabilizer?

How do I take this medicine?

How long do I need to take this medicine?

Is quitting this drug difficult to accomplish?

Are the symptoms likely to return If the medication is stopped? medicine?

Do I need to limit certain foods when I'm taking this medicine?

The following list contains Bipolar Medication

Here are a few of the most effective bipolar medication to test:

Lithium

Lithium is one of the most popular mood stabilizer for those suffering from bipolar disorder. This medication can help in reducing bipolar disorder's "lows" as well as the "highs" that are characteristic of the bipolar disorder. It is also extremely effective in the treatment of manic episodes. It is recommended to be taking this medication for a minimum of two weeks before you start to see the effects.

Lithium, just like every other medication for mental health issues, can cause adverse effects, such as:

Drool

Tremor

Weight loss

Weakness

Diarrhea

Nausea

Memory and concentration problems

The fatigue or weakness

An excessive thirst

Uterine frequency has increased

Stomach pain

When you take lithium, you must regularly conduct blood tests to determine if you're taking the correct dosage. The high doses of lithium can be harmful, therefore you must be cautious. You should undergo the test once a week throughout your initial few weeks of taking the treatment. However, once you've found the correct dosage and you are satisfied, you can have an examination of your blood at least at least every 2 months.

It is important to have regular blood tests since your lithium levels could be affected by many variables, including:

Sodium intake

Weight gain or loss

Tea or coffee consumption

Prescription drugs

The changes in your body's health

To prevent harmful levels from forming You must conduct frequent blood tests. It is also important to cut down on your intake of salt. Additionally, ensure that you drink plenty of fluids, particularly in the summer months and when you exercise.

Valporic Acid

Depatoke, also known as Valporic Acid is an effective mood stabilizer. It is commonly utilized for quick cycling. Valporic acid is a great way to decrease mood swings, and can help you control the symptoms of manic episodes. If you are unable to tolerate lithium, this could be an excellent alternative.

Valporic acid can cause several adverse consequences. It may cause drowsiness, diarrhea, tremors and even weight gain.

Anti Convulsant Medicines

Anticonvulsant medicines are also used to treat bipolar disorder. There are three options: Tegretol (Carbamazepine),

Lamotrigine (Lamictal) as well as Topamax (Topiramate).

Anti Psychotic Drugs

If you are unable to grasp reality, then it could be beneficial to consider taking psychotic medication. Antipsychotic medication can be helpful in the event that mood stabilizers aren't effective for you. You can also mix antipsychotic medication with mood stabilizers, such as lithium and valporic acid.

Here are some anti-psychotic medications that are usually prescribed for bipolar disorder:

Seroquel (Quetiapine)

Zyprexa (Olanzapine)

Geodon (Ziprasidone)

Risperdal (Risperidone)

Clozaril (Clozapine)

Patients who are taking anti-psychotic medication typically experience adverse effects like somnolence, dry mouth, sexual dysfunction blurred vision, constipation.

Benzodiazepines

The majority of mood stabilizers require at minimum two weeks before they begin to work. If you're experiencing an episode of manic and need a medication that is effective immediately You can consider the benzodiazepine. Benzodiazepine is effective within 30 minutes and is a highly effective sedative.

Calcium Channel Blockers

The majority of these medications are used to manage blood pressure, but it also is a mood stabilizer, as well. This is a great option for those who don't like any of the side effects associated with anticonvulsants, or mood stabilizers.

Thyroid Medications

Thyroid dysfunction is common among those who experience fast cycles. The thyroid hormone lithium can lead to low levels, so you might need to take thyroid medication.

Be aware that prior to taking these drugs, you are required to discuss any existing medical issue with your physician. Also, you should talk about your family history particularly in the event that other family members suffer from mental health problems.

Additionally, it is important to keep a notebook and record all your experiences using the medication. Have you experienced any adverse negative effects? Do you believe that the medicines are effective? If not, you need visit your doctor to determine if there are any alternatives.

Chapter 5: Short Stories of Coping and Courage

These are just a few of the stories that my support group have taken the choice to relay to you, so that you will gain a better understanding of the feelings that individuals experience when diagnosed with an illness of the mood. This will help you decide what treatment options are available and the ways that you will manage issues that affect your career, relationships as well as social activities. It also reveals what has been successful for them in dealing with mental illness. The principal focus of this chapter is that we and you fight social stigmas that have been in the forefront of hindering people from seeking assistance. The key to this is the realisation that there is hope in the process of recovery no matter what obstacles stand in the way.

Although it is true that every story, in this instance is distinct and distinctive in their own ways however, they all have the common themes. These are:

Hope- everyone has the conviction that they'll soon be well.

Support- everyone has sought assistance from a broad array of sources. The sources include as well, but are not restricted to, doctors, therapists friends, support groups, and many more.

They are determined to continue looking for the most effective treatment available. This is evident in the level of commitment they display for improving their overall health.

They have all shown their commitment to their treatment plans , despite the obstacles they've encountered and the relapses that are associated with certain drugs.

Before we get into what every bipolar disorder patient is able to share about their experiences it is essential to understand there is no evidence that

Depression and Manic among bipolar patients don't translate into weakness and inability. Instead, we must recognize that bipolar disorder is affecting more than 20 million people around the world. If you follow the right method of treatment, it's possible to treat the symptoms of the condition without having to interfere with your daily life. If you are seeking the treatment you need for your mental health issue, it doesn't mean you are failing at all. It is only a sign that you're resilient enough and possess the courage and the confidence that you are feeling better.

The stories on this page are of diverse patients at various levels of their illness and well-being. One thing to keep in mind is that often it takes various times before a definitive diagnosis can be identified or even before the best treatment is identified for you. There are those who have to attempt various strategies or even wait until the treatment they are receiving is successful. Even though this can be very challenging one of the most crucial things is to keep faith and believing that things will get better. If you're struggling with the same issue as us, don't give up the fight. The most important thing to get back on track is to maintain a positive mindset Be persistent in your quest for the best treatment and assistance from those close to you.

Mercy

Mercy is a girl who has been struggling with bipolar disorder for a long time, without even realizing it. What is striking about her is the fact that she's suffered from depression since the beginning of her childhood. This is evident by the fact that she didn't wish to take any medication. She said that despite the fact that doctors had prescribed medication however, she was unable to accept the pills. But, as she travelled she had to accept her illness and start taking medication for the benefit of her daughter. In the beginning the antidepressants appeared to be effective in controlling her depression until the point at which she was diagnosed with manic depression and had to be admitted to hospital. After years of suffering her illness, she finally received the right diagnosis as bipolar disorder, and received the treatment she required.

What was the solution? A correct diagnosis allowed the doctor to prescribe antipsychotics and mood stabilizers. In addition the medication was successful because of the assistance from her family, her daughter friends, her church and family. As a result the mother and daughter have gained a lot regarding bipolar disorder. While she may have been slipping somewhat because of stress, she is still able to closely work with her doctor to ensure her treatment is successful.

Matthew 19, 19 years old

Matthew is in and out hospital for quite a long period of. In the last few months the doctor noticed he was having a serious manic episode in his college. At the time, he was taking drugs with his buddies when an intense feeling was felt over him. It wasn't the result of the substances they had taken because the effects was already worn off. He recalled that the next day the event, he felt like that he was in the top of the world and had control of everything that was in the universe. He believed that the time he spent sleeping was a waste of time , so the next night he was up writing and reading poems which was a gift the man didn't realize was his. He spent the next day looking for lux things like clothing, shoes food and even treating friends to dinner and lunch. When Matthew returned home, his mother observed that he was bipolar because of his sister who is also bipolar. Then he was admitted by ambulance to the hospital.

What's been successful? According to Matthew the things remain in order as long as the medication he takes. At beginning, he was scared that the medication would alter his personality, which is why the patient was in denial that he had mental illness. Matthew was hospitalized several times because he stopped taking his medication. He was apprehensive about being in the hospital, but he needed to continue taking his medication to heal. Furthermore, when he was having menopausal episodes, he'd talk about things he couldn't be able to revert, and this said, caused him to lose two girlfriends, and, as a result, he turned to taking medication.

With the support of his family doctors, friends and the help of a sister who has bipolar as well, Matthew has managed well. In addition, he has joined the foundation for bipolar sufferers which has proved to be extremely beneficial in helping him get during the accepting phase. He now has a treatment support team that aids him in staying free of substances and stabilizing his moods and medications.

Yolanda Age 44

Yolanda had been adopted by an orphanage located in Japan at the age of year and one-half old. She was a lot neglected at the orphanage, and, as a result she suffered from stunted growth and issues getting around. According to her the trauma she experienced during her childhood was the most significant reason for depression. She tells of her childhood and recorded in her journal that she was a victim of malaria. The reason behind this is the hopelessness that led her believe that she wasn't going to live past the age of. Following the birth of the second baby, she plunged into the deepest depression of her life! When her child was crying in the crib she would be in pain and apprehension. She would recall her childhood being an orphan. She would become annoyed and end up harming herself. After five years she took her own life and was admitted to hospital. This was the time she was given a diagnosis as bipolar.

What's worked? --

She states that she is required to stick to her medication. Her close relationship with her doctor has proved extremely beneficial in making the necessary changes to her medications to lessen the negative side effects , while also ensuring that depression is under control. Friendships with her regularly is a huge help in helping her with treatment and maintaining her mood. She has now become a mom and loves engaging in leisure activities like playing guitar and piano to relax. If she's depressed, she is constantly reminded by her team of support about her positive qualities and the unconditional love she receives from her children.

Mark Age 67, Mark

The first time he was identified with the bipolar disorder in the year 1980. He threw out the entire medication regimen since he was still struggling to been able to accept the fact that he actually was bipolar. On a business trip there was a manic episode. He believed that he could create wings to fly. After he returned back home, his family members wanted to have him admitted to the hospital. The hospital stayed with him for three days, and did his best to pray. Mark was hopeful that when it was over with the hospital, he'd never be afflicted by the illness again. This was when he joined a DBSA the group, which is located in California which he worked with along with his wife to help get groups established to support people who were like Mark.

What's been the result? According to Mark who acknowledged that he had an issue this was the basis for getting the assistance he required. He says that having was surrounded by bipolar disorder sufferers and sharing their stories has tremendously helped him in his recovery. Joining a support group it has transformed his life. The group continues to motivate people by motivating and enthusing people to get better. He is determined to use every means he can to communicate his story to the world, so that people can receive the healing they require, regardless of regardless of whether the public agrees with it or not.

Jane Age 52

When she was a freshman at college, a few years ago Jane began experiencing depressive episodes that negatively affected her academic performance and caused her to drop out of school for a full year. Following her graduation, she experienced a second intense episode of depression which led to her becoming suicidal. She would go through town in search of a place she could buy an assault weapon. At this point, Jane realized that she required assistance and sought help. Jane had been diagnosed as depressed and was prescribed psychotherapy. But, despite that she was not receiving appropriate treatment as all therapy was designed to do was fixing their sexual preferences. A night she was not sleeping and would think of ways to reformulate certain psychiatric theories and bringing this up to her doctor. She was diagnosed with bipolar disorder.

What's been the most effective? It's the reality that she is a certified professional psychiatrist. She is aware that mood disorders do not endure forever and hence playing an essential part in helping her deal to her illness. She is also aware of the various drugs on the market today that pop every day with the aim of helping make her better. This is what motivates her to experiment with the drugs and keep the belief that she could improve her health. Her faith in God has assisted her tremendously in asking God to allow her peace to accept the things she is unable to change. Her partner is also a great source of assistance to keep her aware that she's not failing.

Ricardo, age 60

It was in 1979 that Ric was suffering from the most depressions that he's ever had. However, in the year 1980, he experienced another intense manic episode. In New York, he spent an extended period looking for the correct treatment but was unable to find it. That's when he and his wife thought that the best way to proceed was study other people who had the same condition and how they coped with their illnesses. They founded an organization in 1981 that has grown into an entire organization that helps bipolar patients.

What's been the result? He states that one of the things he's thankful for is that he's not had bipolar episodes for the past 20 years. This, he says is due to excellent treatment by his psychopharmacologist, a supportive wife, dedicated work with a psychologist and his work for the community of people living with bipolar disorder. He says that the most difficult problem is self-stigma and guilt as well as being hypochondriac. But, working to support groups has allowed him to rebuild his confidence and appreciate his leadership capabilities.

Jennifer Age 45, Jennifer

Through the years, it's extremely sad to know that Jennifer was the only child to suffer from temper tantrums and a tendencies to cry without reason at all. She claims that she was known to break almost all the glass she had in her house. The primary reason lies in the fact that she'd get angry over minor things and ruin everything. Then, she would sleep and be at peace. Then, she decided to seek the help of a physician. But her family dissuaded her by telling her that the medication was not a good idea, that the doctors were not qualified and that only if she believed she would be able to get better. She followed their advice and attempted to control the severity of her symptoms on her own. But as time progressed, her situation became worse, and she decided to seek assistance. She saw several doctors before she finally found one who gave her the proper prescription.

What's been the result? According her, the assistance she receives from her partner is unbeatable. He helps keep her up-to-date in the field of bipolar disorder. He also makes sure that she does not stop her medication. Whenever she's feeling unwell she is referred to him.

It is the one who assists her and takes charge of the house and does the household chores. They usually discuss their feelings in a way that they don't get into a situation where they are resentful. Being in contact with her physician is another important factor in her becoming better. With the help of her doctor, she's capable of keeping a journal which allows her to maintain a tracker of her mood which aids in tracking her improvements.

Chapter 6: Value of emotional support and where It's Available

Family and friends are usually the first people who are in your corner to help you navigate through problems. If you suspect that you're not self-regulating, the presence of a friend or family member could be the help you require. While it's not easy to be around someone else all day long, it's not uncommon to have more friends than you'll need in the event that you're open to reaching out to them. Your friends and family around you has a range of ways to support you that will provide the assistance you require.

Religion

For those who are in a manic state, being religious may be the answer, but excessive religiousness can cause issues. It's a difficult decision to make as being on either side could cause harm. The religion of faith is a powerful source of support for those suffering from bipolar. Belonging to a group and being a believer can provide the motivation people require when they're feeling down or struggling and could be the shackle they trust during their manic episodes.

Spirituality helps to build a bond to others, and assists in internal focus, which can assist in improving the way you deal with. Faith can help build a more extensive network of support and offer practical assistance. A lot of faith-based organizations offer 12-step programs and encouraging messages to help those who are who are in need. Many adults who are members of a religious group are more prone to depression. This can lead to being less susceptible to suicide or other harmful behaviours because they don't adhere to the beliefs of that religion.

Writer Julie Fast in her book about Bipolar Disorder, advocates for religion helping you through your suffering. She also believes that being part of a community can act as a buffer to the majority of people.

Improve Self Esteem

It's particularly difficult to believe in yourself when you're not hypomanic to be confident in your self. In these moments when you're in the best position in the world, you're not worried about negatives and are sure. It's hard to imagine being someone who isn't good enough. There are times when you feel like without medication you would not be a whole person. It's all just difficult.

To enhance your thinking in those times of low mood, try to encourage positive thinking. This method of dealing with your thoughts can help to change the words we speak to us, so that we're not as hurtful. For instance, saying that you are "worthless" due to your condition is unfair. It's better to state that it's "struggling". A lot of the labels we make for ourselves are reflections of others however, the illness forces us to believe that it's all our responsibility. Any classification that includes family friends, partners, or family members and their flaws is reflection of their behavior and behaviour and ought to be considered as the case.

Positive thinking is only able to go to a certain extent and is an art that is difficult to learn by yourself. Utilizing a professional therapist to discuss your feelings and thoughts can go a long ways to transforming the way your brain perceives itself. A higher self-esteem level can improve your overall mood and should be nurtured.

Engaging in Yoga for Concentration

Yoga and meditation are fantastic ways to build self-control. A key part of this includes therapeutic breathing as well as the ability to center the mind. This assists in keeping the mind in check, instead of allowing the mind to wander in the manic phase. It's an extremely cost-effective method as yoga and meditation can be done virtually everywhere. It's also a practice that can be practiced on its own, without the help of the assistance of a group, although groups can aid in reducing isolation and establishing connections with others.

The practice of pranayama as well as asana that are based on ayurvedic practices have been found to enhance the way that the bipolar mind functions. Yoga is a fantastic technique for relieving stress depression, anxiety, concentration, easing depression and promoting more wellbeing. There are even yoga studios that provide yoga classes for people suffering from bipolar disorder.

Through improving focus yoga, you can slow down the tendency of the mind to wander off and help bring yourself back once it does occur. This means you'll be much more likely to control your mind whenever you need to and stay motivated during low points. A better focus is essential in overcoming the manic stage. However, isn't yoga an exercise?

Yoga can also be an exercise that is physical, and this will help to release the same chemical similar to other exercises to boost and improve mood. Although many people believe that cardio is synonymous with exercise, this isn't the situation. All physical activities count and by focusing and meditation you're reaping both advantages.

How much?

The practice of yoga, religion or positive thought are essential ways to control your emotions. These can all help alleviate the unpredictable mood changes that are characteristic of bipolar. If you're not religious or you find it difficult to accept the idea then you must look into yoga and meditation as alternatives. There are many Eastern religions that promote the practice, which could be more compatible with your views than the more popular religions.

It is essential to keep your the fervor of religion under control. Certain people be so deeply devoted to their religion that they lose their own faith. Not all religions are secure and certain newer ones can end up being religions disguised as cults. Be sure to consider any decision to adhere to any religion with careful consideration and then decide whether or not it really reflects your convictions.

Example: Maria

She just finished high school and is from a faith-based family. She is concerned that her family does not recognize or support her illness, yet many of her classmates have gone off to go to college. Maria is lonely and disengaged and is unable to manage her issues on her on her own. She goes to an event at the church and realizes there's a group that helps those who are similar to her by praying. She builds a stronger relationship with her faith, and when she's feeling suicidal She reminds herself that she is not doing it right. She relies on her faith and prayers to connect with her God in order to feel less lonely. The church also has the opportunity to take part in a yoga class every week that she participates in. The practice makes her feel more relaxed and less stressed.

Chapter 7: Art Therapy

Methods and treatments commonly employed to treat bipolar disorder can be found in a variety of types and techniques. In the previous sections, this could take the form of smell, or different supplements. However, there are more innovative methods of thinking. In many cases, these unusual approaches have shown excellent results in helping people overcome the negative effects that are associated with bipolar disorder. The form we'll examine in this section that is both unique and efficient and demonstrates the ability of art.

It is a form of treatment that functions as an act of expression. Through this process patients can become more aware of their own issues and those they face. It is said that the American Art Therapy Association defines this type of therapy by defining it as "a psychological health field that allows patients are assisted by an art therapist, employ art-related media as well as the creative process and the resultant artwork, to examine their emotions and conflicts with their emotions and improve self-awareness to control addiction and behavior and develop social skills to enhance their perception of reality, decrease anxiety, and improve self-esteem". This is in line with the goals of this kind of therapy.

Like traditional therapy as with traditional therapy, art therapy helps patients overcome their personal emotional issues. Instead of speaking, patients make artwork to express what they feel. The expression of feelings is linked to numerous advantages, ranging from improved mood and greater self-awareness to less anxiety and a higher self-esteem. These traits are crucial in combating depression, as well as negative feelings and thoughts.

Another reason why art therapy is extremely effective is that often it's difficult for people suffering from disabilities to fully express themselves. This inability to express themselves can result from a myriad of sources However, the ability to help patients overcome their absence of expression can be very satisfying. Art is a place where they can express themselves and express the person they truly are and reflect on how they feel. Since art is typically an expression of mood or the person's mood and attitude, it can easily be examined by a professional therapy. The therapist will then look at the art and attempts to gain a better understanding of the patient's needs by their work. Sometimes this results in patients improving their mood and their mental wellbeing.

One of these instances was with a woman named the Mrs. Robinson. Mrs. Robinson was a 78 year old woman admitted into the nursing home because of her bipolar disorder. This condition made her anxious and she was prone to episodes of extreme anger. Although the majority of conventional methods and treatments were found to be ineffective on her the Ms. Robinson was very responsive to therapy through art. While she did not speak or interact directly with her counselors her work was able to show a steady trend in the course of time. This shift was toward a more optimistic and optimistic perspective on life. When the treatment began the first time, Ms. Robinson's art was chaotic, dark and angry. But, after engaging in art therapy, the paintings eventually got brighter, in line the mood she was in. Following four months of treatment sessions, she received released from the hospital.

The above scenario is only one example however it shows the amazing impact that art therapy could be able to have on bipolar disorder. Self-expression is essential to maintaining a healthy mind since it can help develop a level of self-control that's uncommon in daily life. The feeling of control influences self-esteem, and has been found to be increased through frequent sessions in art therapy.

The use of the art of therapy to be a form of treatment for patients suffering from bipolar disorder has been proven to help patients gain greater understanding of their own issues. The art form, or the process of making artwork, provides patients with the opportunity to think about their life experiences. They also have the opportunity to be in a space of their own in their thoughts and feelings. This is a form of therapy that is beneficial to people who need it. Like self-control, reflection can be utilized as means to improve mood and decrease symptoms of depression or anxiety.

The ultimate purpose in art therapy is enhance or repair the client's performance and their satisfaction with their personal wellbeing. This is accomplished by implementing the techniques described in the previous paragraphs. If you're looking to utilize art therapy, it is important to do it in a setting where you feel comfortable. The main purpose of the therapy is to enhance or improve your functioning and feelings of wellbeing. The kind of art produced doesn't matter as long as the artist is making something of value. If you're participating with art therapy you just create something that's right for you, regardless of whether it expresses your mood, attitude or just what you feel on the day.

Although numerous tests have been conducted on the advantages of art therapy for people who suffer from different illnesses (which include bipolar disorders) There are no adverse results have been reported through the treatment. Because art therapy is not a invasive procedure, and there is nothing being absorbed into the body, it is logical that this is among the least risk-free methods you'll learn about in this book. All you require is paper and a pencil.

Chapter 8: Dealing with The Diagnose: Beware of Stigma and Living Your Life Authentically

"Bipolar disorder can be challenging but it also sets up for you to accomplish almost anything else throughout life. life."(Gluck, "Quotes on Bipolar")

Accepting the Inflammation The Stages

For many will be difficult to get the diagnosis. At first the patient may feel anxious, scared of things to come or some denial. You ask yourself: What's my fault? What was I doing wrong to get this? It's unjust. All of these are normal emotions and thoughts that people suffering from bipolar disorder may experience. It can be difficult to accept that you suffer from a mental illness, and you may need to deal with the effects of it throughout your life. Since, when you suffer from bipolar disorder you have to live daily with the condition from day for many years. There is no cure identified for it, which means you must learn how to live with it and seek out the treatments you require.

There are various stages to acceptance of the disease. It is necessary to go through each stage. These are the steps:

A. Resentment and anger: At this phase, you're angered that you suffer from mental illness. You feel in a hostile way towards God or anyone else or your family members. Your fist is aimed at the wall. You might scream and shout in a fury or even a rage.

B. Refusal: There's nothing wrong with me. I'm perfectly normal! When you are angry with the world, you'll begin to dwell in illusions and believe that there is nothing wrong with your life. It could be that you're just experiencing the beginning of the disease. At first you might be thinking that you'll get through it all on your own.

C. I don't require assistance; I can handle it by myself! In addition to denying the disease, you might be feeling that you're not in need of assistance in dealing with it. Thus, you tackle it on your own. You seek self-medication with drinking, drugs, or other substances because you believe that nobody can assist you in overcoming the problem.

This leads one to the brink where you are at a point of the relapse. Manic episodes may occur in various forms and even mixed state which could be causing you to doubt your ability to keep going on by yourself.

If you have a severe disorder such as depression or mania it is possible to be placed in a mental institution and admitted to an psychiatric institution. It could last from a few several weeks to days or more than the time frame.

D. You visit your doctor once more and confirm the things you've doubted for quite a while. After visiting your doctor, it becomes apparent that something is not right and you'll require assistance.

e. Accepting the necessity for treatment. After having struggled and fretted about the issue for a considerable amount of time, you're determined to address the issue at the highest level of abilities. However, you're aware that you require expert guidance and assistance.

f. Finding an action plan. By consulting with your physician, you are able to create the treatment plan that's appropriate for you. Then, you will be able to follow the steps you need to follow.

G. Keep to your program of care. Once you've created established an agenda, you need to stick to it and follow this program in order to achieve your objectives.

How to deal with the Stigma

The main thing sufferers face with an illness of mental health is the stigma associated with the mental illness. Sharing it with people around you is a challenge to achieve, so you must be cautious when presenting your situation to people around you. Not everyone is going to be able to comprehend the issues you're facing. A lot of people believe that those who suffer from mental health problems are weak and in a position to live full and productive lives. We're here for you to prove that this is completely false and there's nothing to suggest that you're weak when you suffer from an illness that affects your mental health. It's the opposite. You're very resilient and are able to conquer anything you put your mind to.

Don't be afraid of the stigma associated with bipolar disorder. A lot of people are suffering from an issue in their bodies. Certain sufferers have diabetes. Some have weight issues. Perhaps you suffer from bipolar disorder. This condition is not more different than other issues to consider. Take a moment to think about how lucky to have someone capable of rescuing you from the dangers that could be threatening your own. Everyone is our most dangerous adversaries at times. In instances of bipolar disorder it's an "battlefield in the brain. "[1010

Do not worry about what people who are around you will be thinking about how you deal with bipolar symptoms. It is vital that we find methods to reduce stigma associated with mental illness because throughout history mental illness has often been blatantly denied, triggered persecutors, or had other negative results. It is our responsibility to take action to stand in the face of the stigma of mental illness. This is the message that many organizations are launching with. They are raising awareness of mental health issues and problems. Consider the issue of the criminality of mental illnesses. If people could only be aware of mental health issues that cause crime or shootings at schools and in schools, we'd be able to tackle the issues more effectively and let people be peaceful and in peace. It would allow us to prevent large-scale crises in mental health. If people have the freedom to speak about their mental health issues, there will be a lot of improvement in people's attitudes and behavior towards each other.

Living the authentic life with illness

When we've removed the stigma associated with bipolar disorder, we are able to begin to think about how we can be honest about the condition. The definition of authenticity is a level of vulnerability that one must show. It is necessary to be vulnerable in order to make improvements. This is not an easy thing to achieve. It's about being honest with yourself and stating that you'll be able to tackle issues with confidence and with confidence. However, you must acknowledge your limitations. It's not always possible to be able to accomplish everything flawlessly on your own. You'll need help in times and you'll need to accept that the assistance of others is essential to you.

How Hollywood can help to ward off the Stigma

In the past there have been numerous famous individuals with bipolar disorder. Numerous famous actors in Hollywood have been affected by the condition. In the present, a lot of celebrities are working to eliminate the stigma surrounding bipolar disorder. They are determined for bipolar disorder to be more of a visible issue, rather than allowing people to suffer silently. Here are a few examples of famous individuals who are trying to eliminate the stigma.

1. Carrie Fisher

Since she was an aspiring star at the time, Carrie Fisher suffered from numerous trappings that come with fame. Carrie Fisher was plagued by alcohol and drugs addictions. In her early 20s when her doctor informed her she was hypomanic. But she was skeptical about it. After suffering with the illness for a long time it was finally revealed and opened up about the condition as she wrote books about it. For instance Fisher composed Postcards from the Edge and Surrender the Pink. Fisher was among the more open sufferers of bipolar disorder. She continues to discuss the disorder with people in Hollywood. [11She continues to talk about it with people in Hollywood.

2. Linda Hamilton

Linda Hamilton is an actress who has appeared in the Terminator films. She was extremely successful in the film. However, she suffered from bipolar disorder , and was addicted to alcohol and drugs. In the end she was divorced twice due because of the disease. For a total that lasted for 20 years she struggled with the condition. After she was able get help for her disease, she began to talk about the condition. She stated to The Associated Press, "Somebody needs to speak up and let people know that it is okay to discuss it and receive assistance and make use of the resources available (Bhatia 2018, 2018).

3. Jane Pauley

A journalist named Jane Pauley worked for NBC for several years. She appeared on The Today Show, Dateline Today Show and Dateline. When she reached 50 years old she began to suffer from depression and depression and. She wrote about her experience in her memoir Skywriting The Life Out of the Blue. The magazine reported that she said: "If we're lucky, the next generation will not drag through that stigma" (Bhatia 2018.). Pauley was also very vocal in her advocacy for bipolar treatment, and in locating the appropriate medication for each person.

4. Mariette Hartley

This Emmy winning actress Mariette Hartley was a part of many television shows and appeared involved in commercials for a long duration. Hartley had a tough childhood when she lost both her parents and uncle to suicide, while her mother attempted to commit suicide (Bhatia 2018). In 1994 her diagnosis was depression, and afterward ADHD after having suicidal thoughts. The diagnosis was not true. Then the doctor diagnosed her with bipolar disorder. It took her some time to acknowledge her illness however, she was able open about the condition and advocate for those suffering from the condition. She argued for sticking to the correct medication. She advised patients to remain on their medication and not to change to another unless it's not effective (Bhatia 2018, 2018).

5. Catherine Zeta-Jones

Catherine Zeta-Jones is an acclaimed actress, renowned for her performance in Chicago as well as other films. In April of 2011 she was treated to treat bipolar disorder. She was admitted to a mental health clinic , and was there for a brief period to receive the care she required. Catherine Zeta-Jones keeps appearing in the spotlight as a celebrity sufferers of bipolar disorder (Bhatia in 2018, 2018).

6. Demi Lovato

After spending time in rehab for the onset of an eating disorder, and also attempts to harm herself Demi Lovat received a diagnosis with bipolar disorder in the year 2010. She is a rising celebrity who has been quite transparent about her struggles with bipolar disorder, however she has stated in an interview with HuffPost Live that "now, I'm coping well with bipolar disorder."[12[12

After revealing the existence of bipolar disorder Demi Lovato is working to dispel the stigma associated with the condition. However, she is determined to show the world that she's a surviving patient of the illness and she would like people with the condition to be able to live their lives without being judged from society. Her story of triumph should be an inspiration for many.

Bipolar disorder is also used in films. Recently, in Hollywood there have been movies that have featured mental illnesses. In 2016, for instance there was The Ghost and the Whale in which an untreated bipolar patient which causes manic episodes as well as depression (bp Magazine). In the year 2015 Touched with Fire came out, featuring two people suffering from bipolar who fall in love in the mental institution. The film focuses on the love story and the circumstances that led to it. The 2013 film, Repentance, features a man with bipolar disorder. He experiences an immense amount of suffering grieving, loss, and sorrow after the death of his mother. 13

Hollywood has played a significant role in bringing awareness to Bipolar Disorder and the impact on society. It continues to play an important role in helping people get over the stigma that they might face while being affected by the condition. It will also aid people get help when they need it.

Helping others overcome the stigma

Bipolar patients are often viewed as a stigmatized part of society due to being viewed by society as "crazy" and in a position to not become part of society as they are sociopaths who lack social capabilities. People with mental illness is susceptible to discrimination at school, work, and in many other circumstances (Marcia Purse 2018, 2018). The sufferers of bipolar disorder might be targeted for harassment or even directly in front of their faces and behind their backs by people mocking their condition (Marcia Purse in 2018). A lot of people are stigmatized due to the fact that they don't understand the condition and what it means. They may also ignore the issue as it is worthy of attention. Because of lack of understanding and cruelty, many sufferers with bipolar disorder don't want to reveal their condition to other people. This means that many sufferers don't receive the care needed to live happy and fulfilling lives.

Your Responsibility in Informing Others

It is essential as a bipolar sufferer to inform other people about your condition. When people become aware of the condition and its underlying causes they will be more aware of the condition you are suffering from. They'll also not see you as someone suffering from bipolar disorder but instead as someone with ambitions and hopes to achieve in the coming years. Don't allow your bipolar disorder to be your primary characteristic. Your illness is not you. It is important to be aware of this. Even though you may be affected by this condition, it's not a part of who you are. Therefore, you must educate others about the condition so they are aware of the nature of it and what they could do to assist to manage it.

What to Say About Bipolar Disorder

It is also important to be aware of the way you speak about bipolar disorder to your family and friends. Because you're not the cause of your disease, don't mention, "I am bipolar" or, when discussing other people, "she is bipolar." Instead you should state, "I am living with bipolar disorder" or "I am dealing in bipolar disorder." When discussing someone suffering from bipolar disorder, it is best to avoid saying "he's crazy." shouldn't say "he has a mental disorder," or "he has become insane." It is crucial to distinguish the person from the condition. Always speak about it as a matter of possession and not of the person's identity. This can help to view it in a positive light and help you get rid of the feeling of resentment or negativity towards those who suffer from the disease.

Chapter 9: Symptoms Of Bipolar Disorder

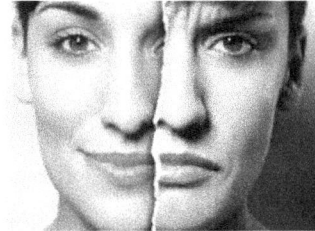

The reasons mentioned earlier appear as a variety of symptoms across different people to show a wide spectrum of bipolar disorder. The depression phase of the cyclic illness manifests in the following symptoms and signs;

Feeling depressed, unimportant or insignificant

Insufficiency of energy. Tiredness. Bipolars are usually tired, even if they haven't done any heavy work. They are burdened on their minds that makes them feel very tired and drained.

Sleeping patterns disrupted. The circadian clock in bipolar patients cannot function properly. The mind can wander to irrelevant things. This causes anxiety, fear , and a insufficient sleep. Awakening early in the morning typically 3:00 am can be a sign of bipolar disorder.

They are thinking very slowly. Psychomotor skills have fallen to their lowest. They're unable to think clearly. It is difficult to concentrate mentally. The blank look is typically the most obvious sign.

There is no desire to be involved in the world surrounding them. They might lose their enthusiasm for sports, news or food or another leisure activity.

Self-worth is low. People may view their worth as insignificant to those who have a wicked view of themselves.

People complain of pains and aches often resulting from injuries that have long gone. The muscles get tighter and cause a variety of discomforts and aches.

Are you not willing to live. Are considering suicide. The person is not connected to the world.

The hypo or mania stage is just the opposite of what we have described above. In the high mood or high-up phase, the person suffering from bipolar disorder experiences the following symptoms.

The feeling of being in the top of the heap. They are very happy and irritable at the same at the same time. This can be a very uncomfortable and uncomfortable high that is good in the beginning stages.

The energy levels during this phase during the cycle can be limitless.the individuals feel they are able to achieve anything.this frequently leads them to over-commit and get into trouble. Sometimes they believe they are just as powerful as God!

The sleep patterns are disturbed. The mind constantly ruminates over the various possibilities, in such a way that it's nearly impossible to rest.

The rate of thought is extremely rapid. In fact, it is so rapid that it is impossible to absorb. Eyes of the patient dance with joy and they can't understand what's happening in the surrounding.

It seems like there is a lot of interest all over the place in an array of different things. Their energy is a huge help to increase their interest in many different things.

Self-esteem is at its peak and they feel they've never been happier. Today, people who are manic are able to conquer the entire world.

All pains and aches disappear quickly and

They believe they will to live for the rest of their lives. They are depressed and experience unstable moods.

The rate of suicide in mania is extremely high. It's about 15 percent. It is higher when symptoms go untreated for a prolonged period of period of time. People with bipolar disorder have trouble maintaining a relationship due to their mood fluctuation. They might resort to street drugs to soothe their anxious mind. Certain patients might begin using alcohol. It is a fact that more than 50 percent of patients suffering from mood disorders are dependent on alcohol. It is important to treat this on its own as a distinct problem.

People who experience lows and highs are extremely imaginative and full of ideas. They are extremely focused and determined. When the lows hit, suddenly everything goes downhill. The ego swells, and the anger, which they have suppressed, turns on themselves which can lead to suicide. This is the reason why there are many suicide hotlines throughout the United States, which function all hours of the day to assist those who need help. They are managed by members who give their time and energy to help the community.

The suicidal idea or desire tends to last a short duration of time. Therefore, if someone is able to take time to talk with them and support them in the time, a lot of deaths could be prevented.

Most often, children who suffered of separation anxiety, or ADHD during childhood are more likely to suffer through bipolar disorder once they reach the teens. It is important to know that certain children have the capacity to overcome situations with a shake their hand , while other children don't. This is the place the place where bipolar disorder takes grips.

Chapter 10: Diagnosing Bipolar Disorder

While bipolar disorder isn't so well-known or recognized as other mental disorders, it's certainly not less when it comes to the consequences and symptoms. In extreme cases, manic depressive episodes can trigger individuals to engage in actions that they aren't used to particularly if they occur in conjunction with hallucinations or illusions. A bipolar disorder that is not treated, diagnosed or treated patient may cause harm to his family members and friends in manic depression attacks.

The only distinction among bipolar disorders and other forms of psychological disorders is the latter is considered to be more manageable and curable provided that a patient is correctly diagnosed and controlled. This is the reason why the majority of cases the diagnosis is crucial in the treatment and recovery of those suffering from bipolar disorder and symptoms.

The American Psychiatric Association (APA) together with other organizations have developed a variety of diagnostic instruments that are designed to establish an unifying language and a standard of definition of psychological disorders like bipolar disorder.

Diagnostic Instruments

The diagnosis of bipolar disorder at first is based on the patient's self-reports and self-observations. It is difficult to recognize if one does not realize that they are displaying signs of depression and mania. Following the patient's own account the next step in diagnosis is based on the experiences of close relatives and friends , as well as the opinions from a psychiatrist, or other specialist within the area of mental disorders.

The primary basis for the criteria used to diagnose schizophrenia within the US is the APA's Diagnostic and Statistical Manual of Mental Disorders fourth edition (DSM-IV-TR). For Europe as well as other regions of the world there is it is World Health Organization (WHO) also has a diagnostic guideline known as"The International Statistical Classification of Diseases and Related Health Problems, version 10.

Apart from psychosocial signs The diagnosis could also include an initial physical examination to identify physical symptoms in the central nervous system, as well as the balance of hormones that could increase the chance of bipolar disorder. The exam is also designed to determine if medical conditions have manifestations are comparable with those in bipolar disorder. These include but are not restricted to hyperthyroidism, chronic illness, and sexually transmitted illnesses like syphilis or HIV.

Imaging and medical scans could also be used to rule out epilepsy or brain trauma. After all other illnesses have been eliminated then following is the process of determine the cause and classify it by using an assessment scale that includes the criteria for classification like Bipolar Spectrum Scale.

Bipolar Spectrum Diagnostic Scale

With this tool, individuals suffering from bipolar disorder are usually divided into different subcategories for mood disorder that fall within that spectrum. These are the mood disorders that are caused by either high or depression-like moods. Here are some codes that are used in this term to indicate the predominant points of Bipolar Spectrum Scale the conditions of a case:

M can be used to refer to an individual with bipolar disorder who exhibits signs of severe manic episodes.

D can be used to indicate the signs of severe or unipolar depression.

The word m can be used to indicate the presence of signs of mania on an insignificant scale (also called hypomania).

D is used to describe the symptoms of mild depression.

The four codes mentioned above can be utilized in conjunction with one another to show mixed symptoms, which are typically seen in those suffering from bipolar disorder. For example the code Md may be a reference to a bipolar person who experiences extreme manic episodes that are accompanied by signs that are mildly depressed.

The order of the letters could also be determined by the sequence in which the patient is experiencing every episode. In bipolar patients the unipolar depression or mania is extremely uncommon. The majority of the time the patients have underlying signs such as depression and mania under an extreme or dominant manifestation or episode.

The scheme can also be employed to recognize other mood disorders that may be closely related to bipolar disorder but are not necessarily linked. Major depression (code D) is one of them. Moreover, experts believe that there's a substantial percentage of the population that is not being diagnosed who suffer from depression (code m) occasionally.

DSM-IV-TR/ICD-10 Classification

Based on the diagnostic tools developed through the APA and the WHO it is possible to determine four main sub-types of bipolar disorders. The sub-types are typically used to define the frequency of episodes and also the kind of episode the patient has experienced in recent times.

This subtype Bipolar I can be used to describe situations where the patient has had at minimum one or more than one manic episode or if the last episode was of a manic variety. In this type hypomanic as well as mild depressive episodes can also occur, although they aren't a requirement to diagnose. Manic episodes are typically caused by psychosis or, in the absence of it, they create an obstacle to the patient's ability to normal activities, such as school or work.

The Bipolar II subtype refers to situations where the patient does not have a history of manic episodes however had hypomanic episodes and major depression episodes. It is important to recognize that hypomanic episodes don't exceed the thresholds of extreme manic episodes, because manic episodes are typically associated with Bipolar I. A lot of Bipolar II patients are mistakenly classified as chronic or major depression due to the fact that patients aren't able to recognize and document the hypomanic episodes they encounter (though this isn't the negligence or fault of the patient's own).

Cyclothymia is an irritable form that is a milder form of Bipolar II which is often associated with frequent hypomanic and depressive episodes that do not qualify as severe, major depression episodes. The term comes from the typical low-grade mood cycles that is for the patient something that is part of his or her character ("being emotional") rather than a characteristic associated with bipolar disorder. The mood swings are typically recognized because they prevent the patient's functioning sometimes.

Bipolar NOS is a term used to describe bipolar disorders that are not explicitly defined. It refers to instances where a person exhibits multi-symptom or mixed symptoms of one or several of the sub-types listed above or if he displays the symptoms of a variety which do not fall to any of the sub-types mentioned above.

Episode Frequency

On average, those who suffer from bipolar disorder can suffer from at the very least 0.4 to 0.7 instances of abnormal moods (mania hypomania, mania, or depression) each year. Each episode could last for a duration of 3 to 6 months.

Most bipolar patients however, are diagnosed with rapid cycle, in which they have at the very least four major episodes each year. Patients may experience rapid fluctuation of moods over one or two days, or even during the same day (known as ultra-rapid cycle).

Related Disorders

The signs mentioned in the preceding chapter and the mood swings that are part of the bipolar spectrum aren't solely associated as bipolar disorder. In reality there are a variety of psychological disorders that could have similar symptoms. Here are a few of them, along with their distinctions with bipolar disorder.

Schizophrenia is a psychiatric condition in which the patient suffers mental disturbances and the inability of generating emotional reactions. The most typical symptoms of the condition are auditory hallucinations ("hearing voices") and paranoia and delusions. Bipolar patients who experience intense mood swings or depression may be mistaken for schizophrenics.

A condition known as Dissociative Identity (also known as Multi-Personality Disorder) is a rare psychiatric disorder in which an individual's behavior is guided by one or two distinct identity and different ones. The presence of multiple personalities isn't recognized since patients are often affected by memory loss as the change of personality occurs. This isn't caused by drug consumption. It is also difficult to identify because it is usually associated with other mental problems. Bipolar patients may have similar symptoms, particularly since they are afflicted by two extremes in their energy and mood.

The Borderline Personality Disorder (BPD) is a mental disorder that is often associated with high and unstable moods such as impulsivity, self-esteem, and impulsiveness. People suffering from BPD are extremely fearful of being hurt emotionally or abandoned by those they love Some may also exhibit suicidal behaviors and causing harm to themselves.

Attention Deficit Hyperactive disorder is an emotional disorder that is characterized by difficulties in an individual's ability to focus, impulsivity or even hyperactivity that is not normally regarded as normal. ADHD is typically found in children between the ages of 6-12 years old. The hyperactivity in people suffering from ADHD may be similar to hypomanic or manic episodes experienced by people suffering from bipolar disorder.

Bipolar disorder may lead to the development of additional psychiatric disorders as a type of complications if not treated. Apart from the disorders listed above, other disorders that can be co-existent with bipolar disorder include panic disorders as well as obsessive compulsive disorder.

Famous Bipolar Individuals

Bipolars are distinct from psychopaths and other people with an antisocial personality. While some bipolars may be convicted of crimes in the middle of a hallucinatory experience however, many are high-functioning people who are considered to be experts and experts in their area of expertise. Psychologists have suggested that high-functioning capability is linked to hypomanic episodes.

Some bipolar people you might recognize , or admire include Ludwig Van Beethoven, Amy Winehouse, Edgar Allan Poe, Florence Nightingale, Catherine Zeta Jones, Vincent Van Gogh, Sidney Sheldon, Mel Gibson, Frank Sinatra, Virginia Woolf and Jean-Claude van Damme.

Chapter 11: Depression: What Is, and How To Find It

A different emotional state is depression, also known as an episode of depression, and they are not less serious than manic episodes. The depressive episodes are characterised by extremely low levels of mood and a persistent feeling of gloominess and despair. Some people have described depression as well as depressive episodes as feeling burned out, exhausted and slowing down.

These episodes occur when at minimum five of the symptoms below are felt almost every day for at the very least two weeks.

Feelings of despair, sadness and frustration.

A persistent and substantial deficiency in energy

Fatigue/tiredness, regardless of the intensity of work or physical activity Particularly in the morning

- Significant anger, agitation or anger

Changes in appetite and the weight (loss or increase)

Tendency belief in negative thoughts (e.g. "I'm useless/insignificant", "It's my fault" etc.)

Suicidal behavior and thoughts

People who are depressed or suffering from depressive symptoms are also experiencing a decrease in their ability to manage even the most basic of tasks. Most often, they are overwhelmed by anxiety, tears or anger when faced with small conflicts or making the need to make a decision.

In extreme cases of depression, people might also experience episodes of psychosis (e.g. hallucinations or delusions).

The same applies to should you experience any of these symptoms and symptoms, you must pay attention to the signs. Often, early detection of symptoms is the best way to stop an entire episode from occurring because it allows your loved ones to receive the appropriate medications and preventative measures to help stabilize the condition.

Although they are less severe hypomania and hypomanic episodes are still emotional states that you need to watch out for.

The HYPOMANIA Virus: What is it? AND HOW DO I IDENTIFY IT

Hypomania is usually referred to as an "middle state" which isn't as serious as depression or mania. Although it's not as serious however, hypomania is still a risk because it is susceptible to rapidly changing into depression or mania.

Hypomania is characterised by a strong feeling of wellbeing, strength as well as general feeling of euphoria , or happiness. The people who suffer from hypomania also experience an increase in their sensuality and senses. This can lead to the desire to engage in sexual activities to satisfy these physical cravings.

Hypomanic episodes occur when your loved ones experience increased mood levels along with three of the signs listed below for at the very least four days. A different definition of an episode of hypomanic is irritation and some of the indicators described below, which lasts for at most four days.

Here are the indicators:

A higher level of self-esteem confidence, grandeur, and belief in one's strengths and abilities

A decrease in the need for sleep

Experience a flash of inspiration that are mostly grand or creative (these events are thought to be less serious than those experienced in the mania)

Arousal from the mind, or an unproductive series of physical movements that originate from tension and anxiety (e.g. the pacing, scratching or picking on the skin, using nails etc.)

Lack of focus/inability to focus on tasks in hand

Engaging in activities that are likely to trigger emotional or psychological stress (e.g. inappropriate sexual acts, sex-seeking, recklessness, etc.)

Hypomania can be difficult to detect, considering that symptoms are benign with a general positive outlook. So, the most essential thing to do is be aware of the negative signs that are related to hypomania (as well as other mood disorders that are associated with bipolar disorder) such as excessive impulsivity, difficulty in focusing, adverse sleeping patterns, psychomotor agitation and others.

For depression and mania It's crucial to alert them to the negative signs to allow them to act promptly and prevent hypomania from transforming into depression or mania.

These kinds that occur are typical to diverse forms of bipolar disorders, and we'll examine in the next section. It is helpful to understand the specifics of each type because it will make it easier to search out for patterns of behavior that indicate risk or instability.

Types of BIPOLAR DISORDER

Apart from understanding the various emotional states your loved one is experiencing, it's essential to understand what each type of bipolar disorder has. Understanding the different forms at the very least can help you to identify particular patterns of behavior that indicate instability or danger.

Here are the various kinds that bipolar disorder can be able to take:

BIPOLAR I DISORDER

If you know someone who suffers from Bipolar I disorders, they typically experiences severe moments of mania or depression. This kind of disorder is also referred to as manic depressive disorder, with people who have had at most an episode of manic. It is important to note that, in between these episodes, individuals can perform their normal activities every day.

BIPOLAR II DISEASE:

The form that this one is identical to Bipolar I, since patients with Bipolar II disorder also experience changes in mood and emotions. The difference is that , if you have a loved one classified as Bipolar II disorders, they'll be experiencing hypomania, not full-blown manic episodes. This means that they have experienced at the very least one hypomanic episode in their lifetime. As with Bipolar I, people who suffer from

Bipolar II can function normally between depression episodes and hypomania.

CYCLOTHYMIC DISEASE:

In comparison to other types in bipolar disorder this kind is thought to be relatively mild. The people who suffer from cyclothymia have fluctuations between brief bouts of hypomania and mild depression. These mood swings are not as traumatic as the mood swings suffered by people who suffer from bipolar disorder. This is why cyclothymic disorder is usually regarded as only one of the "bipolar-like" condition.

RAPID CYCLING BIPOLAR DISEASE

The condition is defined as having at least four mood-related episodes (mania depression, mania or hypomania) which occur during the course of twelve months. If you have a loved one diagnosed with this disorder it is likely that they'll experience extreme mood swings in short time periods and may experience changes within a single day or even a week. This type of condition is thought to be quite extreme, and sufferers are at the possibility of developing suicidal ideas or ideas, as well as behavior.

Due to how prone to this kind of behavior is why it's essential to be aware of these rapid mood swings. It's safer than regretting, so don't sit around waiting for this behavior to go indefinitely without any intervention for any period of time.

Chapter 12: Bipolar Disorder And Relationships

The majority of the time when a mental issue interferes with relationships. Being bipolar is no exception. As if it wasn't difficult enough to recognize the individual's mood swings and manage risky behavior it is also important to think about other people who are who are significant to the individual.

If someone is suffering from bipolar disorder, it can be difficult to maintain relationships in the long-term. There will be occasions that the person is unable to keep his or her anger in check and there is a good likelihood that they will snap at someone who is in close proximity. In one instance, the person suffering from bipolar disorder is in a good mood and the two of them are having fun, and then suddenly, the person gets angry and snap at the person in the opposite direction. The person who was offended is likely to seek forgiveness with regard to the incident but both partners will end up within the same circle within a few days. The question is, who would want to be in the relationship?

If both parties recognize that the issue isn't the individual (with bipolar disorder) who suffers from the disorder, but rather that there an issue with the mind to be considered it is a chance the two parties will be able to keep their relationship. The process of preserving relationships, in the end requires trust, concern and understanding of all the parties. The parties involved should let go of the relationship. Being in an intimate relationship with bipolar people just requires an extra amount of effort than other normal relationships. Each party must put in some effort for the relationship to last.

Awareness

Both parties must be aware that one of the people within the relationship is suffering from mental illness. This is when those who are caring for the person suffering from the disorder will manifest. When they are aware that the loved one is suffering from bipolar disorder they can find ways to reduce the individual's unpredictable behavior to the other person.

However being aware of the person suffering from bipolar disorder will aid the person to put in effort in regulating one's emotions and behavior. Being aware of the presence of bipolar disorder is a premise that both parties need to have to make it more easy for them to recognize and manage any the bipolar disorder-related issue that could occur.

Understanding

For people suffering from bipolar disorder, it's difficult to comprehend the real cause. This is more difficult for people who have to manage the person suffering from bipolar disorder. Anyone who is not affected must realize that those suffering with mood swings doesn't necessarily feel in control of their behaviours and emotions. It may seem unfair to someone who doesn't suffer from the disorder however, try to sympathize with the other person as they are suffering from many things.

The person who has the disorder should realize that everyone has limitations and that should they be unable to alter or lessen the behavior inconsistencies the likelihood is that the person with the disorder will be frustrated.

Forgiveness

Everyone makes mistakes. Everyone is not perfect. There are a lot of mood swings that are going to happen during one day. Some people will be angry and others are unable to endure but at the end If both of them remember that the things spoken and done was not the fault of the person , but due to their illness it is much easier to accept each other's forgiveness. However, this does not mean that mental illness can be used into a reason for any thing that the person suffering from the disorder has done.

Bipolar disorder sufferers should be aware that there are certain items that can be considered unacceptable regardless of one's mental illness. A normal person is also advised to define limits for those suffering from the disorder, so that they are aware of what they should not do. So, certain actions could be done and said but there is room to forgive.

Support

The normal person within the relationship should be encouraging the other partner to get to a doctor. It is more beneficial for the person suffering from bipolar disorder feels that they are being assisted by the other person. Inspiring the person to the doctor, accompanying the person to therapy (there is psychoeducational therapy for couples that is available) and reminding the person of what to do regarding the treatment for the disorder are methods to help the person who suffers from the disorder feel like they are being supported.

Being with them through their ups and downs can be a huge help to those suffering from the disorder. It doesn't necessarily mean only the normal person is required to give all the love and support to the relationship. Bipolar patients is expected to perform the same. A normal person will also have their own downs and ups (although they are less prominent as those who suffer from bipolar) and being around the person who has bipolar disorder will have a huge impact on them.

Like normal relationships and the relationship between a "normal" person and one suffering from bipolar disorder is exactly the same and requires the same efforts from both parties.

Chapter 13: What are the Treatments for Mdd?

The psychotherapy

The duration of two of the most popular options for psychotherapy is brief: 12-20 sessions. They seek to alleviate depression symptoms through Inter-Personal Therapy (IPT) and Cognitive Behavioral Therapy (CBT). Research has shown that both aid in relieving symptoms, in contrast to the use of medications. Patients with mild to moderate symptoms have an excellent initial response to each psychotherapy (14).

CBT blocks negative and disorganized thoughts about the self, future and life. These distortions lead to behaviors which often accompany depression episodes and can even exacerbate the symptoms. Through CBT, the patient is taught to recognize and alter negative and untrue thoughts. As a result, behavior shifts, which is a major factor in improving mood (14).

In the same way the patient is urged to keep doing activities that satisfy. This is crucial since patients tend to avoid the activities that are not satisfying. This is known as the change in behavior (BC). Thus, even in the face of problems, the individual is enticed to keep up their routines. If the person is unable to continue do it, be patient and allow him/her opportunity to return to them (14).

IPT aids in the overcoming of issues in relationships. If they are not addressed, these issues may lead to depression. Being able to rely on emotional support can be helpful to recover from a depression episode. Troubleshooting therapy provides effective and direct assistance by identifying and subdividing difficult areas into smaller tasks. This is how one can learn strategies to address specific problems. Each one by one, they can be resolved quickly. Additionally breathing techniques as well as the known as progressive relaxation can be very beneficial. Progressive relaxation concentrates on relaxing and contracting certain muscles. The tension in muscles is common among the majority of depressed individuals.

What is the best the medication?

There is no need to be worried about medicines!

What if you feel overwhelmed, depressed and in danger of taking your own life instead of taking the antidepressant? Do you think it's an uneasy decision to make? Many people believe that depression can be able to improve with the absence of "dangerous" medications for the brain! Data from epidemiology show about 15% depressed patients attempt suicide. They kill fewer people than the illnesses they treat. The same is true for medications generally in all medical areas! It is important to admit it and be truthful about it.

Like all things on earth, people must weigh the pros and pros and. When a doctor prescribes a medication that has benefits, they must be greater than the risk. There are many who are against taking psychotropic medications (drugs that treat problems with CNS, the brain and central nervous system., also known as CNS). They claim that they are addictive. I'm with them! It is addictive in the same way that patients suffering from other ailments depend on medications that combat them. Below are a few instances.

Hypertension (high blood pressure) requires a continuous treatment with antihypertensive medication. The condition must also be treated throughout the course of one's life. Of course, we're talking about the vast majority of patients that's the type of dependency we've discussed. Don't mix "healthy dependence" and "dependency" which helps save life with "unhealthy addiction" that is morally indefensible.

For psychotropics, many people consider these with the label "addictive." Like nicotine, alcohol or other illicit substances (e.g. cocaine, marijuana). These drugs can destroy your health and your life. Psychotropics can give you your health and vitality back! There is no prejudice against the use of psychotropics for other health conditions, for instance for heart problems. Even if the medicines are used for the duration of a lifetime. However, almost everyone is against treatments for mental health illnesses, including patients who are taking these medications!

It is typical in my office hearing from my patients saying that they do not wish to be on medication for long periods of time, or even throughout their lives even though they are taking various medications for different medical issues without complaining and even throughout their lives. Modern medicine has improved the amount and quality of the years that are lived. 100 years ago, the majority of the population's lifespan was just 30 years. In today, in the majority of the nations the population lives for either around 80 to 90 years!

There were people who died from any health issue, however simple it may be. Today, many individuals suffering from diabetes, high blood pressure or cancer AIDS and more. are able to live for a long time and lead full, active lives. What is the difference for those who suffer from mental illness? For all medical conditions, including psychiatricdisorders, drugs are an element of treatment. It's just as important as the non-medical interventions. It is vital in the case of other treatments.

The wise and educated could not deny it? Does treating hypertension using combined strategies not much better? Combining an antihypertensive medication with physical exercise, diet and relaxation techniques can lead to improved outcomes. Remember that those who "depend upon" any medication can be rehabilitated. The effects of diseases decrease the lifespan and level of living.

You have the option of choosing. You can either leave your life "according to" what the disorder does of it and "depend to" the treatment that gives you the control of your fate. It's that easy! Each decision must be based on both the positive and negative aspects. It's a good idea! Doctors who are good at their job don't expose patients to medications which cause more pain than the disease. It's a good thing he doesn't do this!

To begin taking a medication, it is important to think about:

The symptoms that are present

The dangers of drinking alcohol while driving

The adverse negative effects

The evidence of improvement after taking this drug (in the person who is depressed or family members)

The cost of finance

The antidepressants all have the same effectiveness. The main difference is the adverse effects that the various. One of the main difference is the chance of overdose or poisoning, particularly with prescriptions for those who are at risk of suicide. The latest antidepressants are less toxicities and are simpler to regulate the dose (15 and 16).

Antidepressants: Aspects of Antidepressants

We would like to discuss the most important features of an antidepressant. Both the patient and doctor must share responsibility to select the appropriate treatment. It's not you that is prescribing! This information will allow you play an active and deliberate part in deciding on the most effective medication, in conjunction with your physician.

It is not our goal to inform you in complete details about the treatments. It is the duty of the doctor. The knowledge gained by physicians is acquired through the course of their studies which includes Six years of undergraduate studies followed by four years education in the field of psychiatry. It's at least ten years of education! Do you now realize how difficult to find a suitable prescription be? This is the reason why the prescribing of a medicine (in our case, an antidepressant) isn't a straightforward job, as some imagine! It is best to be careful when we prescribe a drug. Don't attempt to self-medicate, or locate an individual prescription. Talk to a doctor for guidance.

SSR Inhibitors (SSRI)

These are the first option for treating depression. The SSRI are considered safe when used in large amounts, such for instance, in those who try suicide.

The most frequent adverse side effects are:

Nausea

Insomnia and lack of appetite

Weight loss

Extreme sweating

Nervousness

Insomnia

Sexual issues (decreased desire and difficulties in sexual stimulation and orgasm)

Sedation

Afflicted fatigue

Vertigo or dizziness

Rare side effects include:

Dry mouth

Constipation

Bleeding issues

Nighttime bruxism (teeth grinding)

Hair loss

Recent memory issues

The effects of the side effects fade after a couple of weeks when the body is familiar with the medication, or at the majority of them.

The longer the time it takes to get the dose established, the less negative side negative effects.

SSRIs aren't toxic (hazardous) for the blood pressure or heart.

The daily maximum and starting doses for each drug in the members of the SSRI family of medications are:

Fluoxetine 20 mg or 80 mg

The 20-mg and 80 mg doses of Paroxetine

Citalopram 20 mg, and 80 mg

500 mg Sertraline, and 200 mg

Escitalopram 10 , 40 and 20 mg

Fluvoxamine 50 mg and 400 mg

Serotonin, and Norepinephrine Reuptake Inhibitors (SNRI)

These include duloxetine and venlafaxine. They are extremely effective and safe when used in large doses, and they are not harmful on the cardiovascular system. They are especially effective in dealing with physical symptoms of depression like pain.

Common side effects:

Nausea

Insomnia and lack of appetite

Weight loss

Extreme sweating

Nervousness

Insomnia

Sexual issues

Sedation (somnolence)

Tiredness (Cinch)

Headache

Dizziness

Venlafaxine in large doses can result in an elevation in blood pressure.

The maximum and initial dosages per day are as follows:

Venlafaxine XR 37.5 mg and 300 mg

Duloxetine 30 mg or 60 mg, 120 mg or 180 mg

Tricyclic antidepressants (TAD)

They also include drugs like:

Amitriptyline

Clomipramine

Nortriptyline

Imipramine

Desipramine

They've been in use for many years and are a good value. Due to their adverse side consequences and high heart toxicity, they should not the best choice for treatment. They should be avoided for patients who are who are at high risk of suicide.

The most frequent adverse effects include:

Dry mouth

Constipation

Urinary retention

Tachycardia (fast heart rate)

Vision blurred or double vision

Memory issues

Sedation

Affections are rising

Gain in weight

TADs may enhance the effects of drugs that depress on the central nervous system. They may cause postural hypotension. If you stand quickly you might feel dizzy and have the reflex of tachycardia (accelerated pace of heart) because of a decrease in blood pressure. This effect is particularly hazardous for seniors due to the possibility of falling and fractures. To prevent it, simply shift the position from one to the next (e.g. lying, to standing and sitting) gradually.

TADs may increase the effects of antihypertensive medication It is important to be taken when combined. The blood pressure can drop abruptly with serious negative consequences. Certain of these medications are:

Prazosin

Terazosin

Doxazosin

Labetalol

Certain patients shouldn't use TAD in the event of pre-existing health conditions:

Cardiac conduction (arrhythmias)

Angle-closure glaucoma

Prostate hypertrophy

The adverse effects go away after a few weeks particularly if we increase our dosage slowly. If you are required to use the TAD it is a matter for the supervision of someone else. Someone else should provide the drug the TAD to you and then store the drug.

Before beginning treatment with TAD We conduct the electrocardiogram (EKG) and then repeat it after four weeks. This test is performed due to the potential impact of TAD on the heart.

People suffering from insomnia as well as losing appetite or body weight loss benefit from using TAD. Many of the adverse effects are helpful in these instances. However those who experience drowsiness and an increase in appetite and body weight can be aggravated by these drugs. In these situations, an alternative antidepressant must be prescribed.

Antidepressants that are atypical (AA)

They include drugs like:

Bupropion

Mirtazapine

Trazodone

Nefazodone

The effects of side effects can vary based on the drug. They are generally safe when taken in large doses, but there is a small adverse impact to the heart.

Common adverse effects of every AAinclude:

Bupropion:

Agitation

Insomnia

Weight loss

Dry mouth

Headache

Constipation

Tremor

Seizures. Four out of 1000 patients, particularly those taking more than 450 mg per day.

Rarely, it causes sexual dysfunction. In fact, it could help to reduce this side effect that is caused by SSRIs.

Mirtazapine:

Sedation. It is commonly utilized in conjunction with other medications to help with insomnia.

The sensation of a snoring

Affections are rising

Gain in weight

Dry mouth

Constipation

Dizziness

Trazodone:

Sedation

Orthostatic hypotension

Headache

Heart rhythms can be a problem for those who suffer from heart disease

It is a an ongoing penile erection. It is an uncommon, but serious issue

Nefazodone (Serzone):

The sensation of a snoring

Dizziness

Dry mouth

Nausea

Constipation

Headache

Amblyopia (decreased vision acuity in either eye or both)

Blurred, double or even blurred vision

It could cause fulminant hepatitis. It is recommended to avoid it in patients suffering from liver impairment. We must monitor the levels of liver enzymes in blood.

Monoamine Oxidase Inhibitor (MAOI)

The drugs are prescribed to treat atypical depression the symptoms of which are:

No or little sadness

The loss of energy

The sensation of a snoring

An increase in appetite

Weight loss

Extremely sensitive to rejection

A highly intense reaction to any external stimuli. For example, someone might have a crying moment, yet then bursts out laughing at the sound of an absurd joke. Someone suffering from MDD is not affected in exactly the same way. This type of intense reaction is more frequent in bipolar depression than MDD.

Patients who are resistant to other treatments can also benefit from using MAOIs. Be cautious when taking MAOIs because they can cause:

Meperidine and drug interactions (an opioid herring medication used to ease pain).

The possibility of a fatal hypertension is in the event of an interaction with food that contain Tyramine. Tyramine is a compound that is present in certain food items, like:

air-dried meat

matured or fermented animal products

sausages or salami

Herrings that have been picked

Anchovies

Liver

red wine

beer

aged cheeses

blue

brick

cheddar

parmesan

romano

Swiss

milk cream

sauerkraut (vinegared cabbage)

fig syrup

dried figs

raisins

Bananas and avocados (especially when they are the fruit is ripe)

Soy

soy sauce

Tofu

shoyu sauce

Bean curd

broad beans

yeast extracts

Alcohol can cause some adverse effects on the central nervous system:

Dizziness

Nosoilence

It is difficult to concentrate

It can cause serotonin-related syndrome when it is combined with SSRI as well as other serotonergic medications. The syndrome may be the cause of:

Heart attack

Vascular collapse

Fever

Tachycardia

Even death

The most commonly reported adverse effects include:

Insomnia

Sedation

Orthostatic hypotension

Gain in weight

Sexual dysfunction

The most common side effects are:

Tremors

Vision double/blurred or blurred

Dry mouth

Constipation

Urinary retention

During the course of treatment for depression certain situations can occur (Figure 1) The Figure illustrates the phases of therapy from beginning to the end and also its negative consequences.

Figure 1. A Kupfer (17) chart of the course of treatment for depression.

Treatment phases:

Acute is a condition that lasts for up to 4 months. The goal is to achieve the state of being that is the reduction of symptoms for 50% of. Relapse is the deterioration of the symptoms after initial relief.

Continuous - lasts for 4 or 12 months. It's the remission phase that is the total improvement in the symptoms. In this stage the patient is able to resume his normal life. As in an acute state, in this phase we refer to the relapse when symptoms return.

Maintenance lasts for longer than 12 years. It is designed to stop the repetition of episodes. Recurrence occurs when a new depression episode occurs after you are completely recovered, and functioning.

The alleviation of the symptoms (response) during an acute stage, even if it is only partial, is the first stage. After that, symptoms are completely gone (remission) in the ongoing phase. It is important to avoid relapses of symptoms during the acute phase and the continuation phase. In the maintenance and the continuation phases, patients should be able return to normal activities. The time comes that the patient is able to recover from the depression episode. The continual use of antidepressants is to stop the occurrence of new crises which is known as recurrences or relapses.

We can assess whether we've achieved our goal by following:

The patient can himself feel better on a scale from between 0 and 10. Zero is the state of the patient prior to the start of treatment. Ten means a 100 100% recovery.

Self-assessment scales are used. They are used prior to or during treatments. They track the progress through time. Psychologists and doctors have a variety of them available.

The observation of people who reside in the same house with them, like relatives, friends, or colleagues. Usually, these people observe improvements even before it's acknowledged by the person who is depressed.

If the patient is feeling better and has returned to routine activities, we can provide the best evidence of a successful treatment.

Chapter 14: Living Joyfully With Bipolar

There is no reason to not live a fulfilling and joyful life, regardless of whether you're diagnosed with bipolar. Remember that you are able to manage and regulate your mood. Here are the top self-help techniques and strategies that you can employ to maintain your balance.

Learn to Know Your Symptoms Well

If you are aware of and comprehend your symptoms You can take action to prevent them from happening again. Be aware of small or subtle changes in your mood, feelings or mood. Most of the time, prior to your depressive or manic episodes there are signs by subtle mood shifts.

Recognizing these changes will allow people to adopt preventive measures to prevent a full-blown depression, mania or both. Pay attention to warning signs, and then follow these steps to avoid an onset of bipolar disorder that is severe:

Stop for a short break from your routine. Find a peaceful location and time when you can unwind your body and mind.

Focus your attention on healthy actions and thoughts. Chat with a trusted friend who can provide an open ear, without judgement or arguing with you, or denying the things you say.

Sometimes, by the simple act of clearing those negative thoughts or feelings you could be able to stop your mood fluctuation.

If you've been drinking cigarettes or alcohol and cigarettes, you should avoid these. They only aggravate your illness. People with bipolar disorder who smoke or drink would be better off kicking these bad habits and vices.

Follow the prescribed dosage of your medication. If you do not think your body responds to natural remedies in a positive way ask your doctor regarding the possibility of reducing the dose of medicine. It is recommended that you switch from traditional treatment with drugs to natural.

Connect on your support system in order to keep you on the right path. Your support system is an invaluable resource in keeping you focused on winning your fight against this disorder. They will give you solid and healthy tips, act as your listening ear aid in diverting your attention to positive and hopeful thoughts to positive thoughts and productive pursuits, help reduce stress and stop your delusions from becoming a reality.

Triggers and Signs

Be on the lookout for these for these common triggers and can alert that you are experiencing an episode of depression or mania, or both of them:

Stress and anxiety

Arguments that aren't necessary with people whom you love

Financial difficulties and issues

Troubles sleeping and sleep

Weather conditions change

If any of the above are present, note the way you are feeling. Keep a journal in which you write down the changes you notice in your moods, emotions or mood. This will help you discern patterns in the mood swings or shifts.

Make Your Own Arsenal Against Bipolar

The amount of time you have is crucial in fighting off and preventing episodes of depression and mania. It is therefore essential that you have your arsenal of weapons to protect yourself from the affliction.

There isn't a universally-fit-all arsenal for bipolar disorder. Each person is a unique individual with a individuality, which is why must create an arsenal tailored to each person's particular needs and circumstances.

Here are a few essential weapons you can play with or mix:

Create a chart of symptoms that will keep track of your symptoms

Keep a record of your journal, whether digital or manual

Pause from your daily activities

Beware of the triggers and causes of anxiety and stress.

Join a bipolar support group for bipolar

Speak to someone you love or a trusted friend

See your doctor or counselor

Relax, de-stress, and unwind

Make sure you get enough rest

If oversleeping, cut back

Intensify your physical activity or decrease them if are nearing an episode of manic.

Use your thoughts to create something useful and inspiring

Limit your consumption of smoking and alcohol.

Limit your consumption of caffeine and sugar.

Start at a very early hour in the morning to capture the morning sun or boost the amount of light exposure

Consume healthy foods, e.g. instead of eating unhealthy food items, have a snack of fruit salads or a bowl of fresh vegetables

Participate in art or painting lessons to be a source of therapy

Participate in singing or dancing lessons, which can be relaxing.

Spend time with your friends or family members and request their moral and emotional assistance

Making an emergency Course of Action

Sometimes, your episodes might catch you off security, or you might get into a relapse, or even an unbearable circumstance. From now on prepare for this possibility and be prepared with your alternate plan of taking action.

The action plan could comprise the following:

Prepare a list of emergency contact numbers (hospital or doctor, therapist and family members, etc.) and supply your support system with these numbers.

Create a list of the prescription medications you're currently taking, if you are able to. put it up somewhere that your family members or close family members can look up during emergencies.

Your family members should be provided with vital information about your health conditions, which may influence the treatment for your bipolar disorder.

Any other details or directions that could aid others to take the appropriate action in your crisis.

Develop and nurture relationships that are beneficial to you.

A strong support system is essential to living a happy life despite your circumstances. Humans are social creatures, and you're not an exception. Find people who can help you conquer your depressive or maniatic episodes Avoid negative people who could drag you down, only to increase or worsen your symptoms.

Here are some ideas be sure to have a positive environment with those who will be positive and happy:

Remember that a reliable support system starts with your the home. Your family members are the ideal people to offer you the necessary and crucial support to win your battle with bipolar. They play a significant role in keeping or restoring your equilibrium and steady mood.

Be in touch with your family and your friends. Be sure to not isolate yourself, instead, go out with your friends and family. The idea of locking yourself in your home and avoiding contact with your people you know can only intensify the severity of your depression.

Join communities or support groups for bipolar sufferers. These are groups comprised of individuals who have been with the same illness like you and are now recovering and living normal lives, and people experiencing a similar illness to yours.

Find new friends and begin a an enjoyable and mutually beneficial relationship with them. To achieve this, you must get out of your lonely building and discover the world. Find organizations that are in your area which you could join. Meet with your neighbors. Donate to charity.

Tips for Building and nurture relationships

Stop blaming. Don't blame anyone else as well as yourself, for your mess that you find yourself in. Accept the fact that bipolar is a condition and is treatable and manageable.

Learn to be an effective listener. Bipolar individuals tend to dominate the conversation and make their listeners feel overwhelmed by their worries. Change the subject and understand that conversations are not just one-way, which means you have to be attentive.

Every day, do something that you're afraid of doing because you are worried about your situation. For instance, Join a club, contact an acquaintance you haven't had contact with in many years, or invite someone over for dinner or lunch.

If you're not feeling well, you should rest. Don't force yourself to meet with people or engage in a conversation, or email someone if you feel that things are not going well for you. But, don't nurture your illness because it could trigger an episode. When you've had enough sleep take a productive action, e.g. get rid of the clutter around your bedroom or at your bedside.

Make small, achievable goals that are realistic and achievable. It can take some time to overcome and overcome your bipolar disorder. Smaller goals for building relationships are more achievable than goals with a large scope.

The small accomplishments you make can be a source of motivation to achieve bigger goals to the final goal of being satisfied and free of your manic depression.

Minimize Your Stress

Stress is the primary trigger for manic depression episodes. You must learn to manage stress trying to control the symptoms of bipolar disorder, and enjoy living with the disorder.

Bipolar disorder doesn't have to be a weapon in your back. one approach to ward it off is to manage stress and keep it at the bare minimum. Here are a few most effective methods to reduce stress and eliminate it:

Deep breathing - Take an unintentional break from whatever you're doing and perform 5 minutes of deep breathing.

Relax in a comfortable chair and you'll feel at ease. Put your head down. Place one or both hands on your stomach. Take a breath slowly through your nostrils, bringing the breath from the belly and extending to your head. Inhale slowly with your mouth.

This exercise will relax your nerves, reduce your heart rate and reduce your blood pressure.

Be present - Engage in activities and things that bring you happiness. Enjoy a good film with your friends or your family. Take a sniff of the flowers. Relax and enjoy your preferred music. Savour the delicious flavor of your dinner.

Just five minutes to slow down and be present in the moment could help in reducing stress levels and preventing the symptoms of bipolar from starting an episode.

The ability to laugh is possibly the most effective therapy. the most appealing aspect of the ability to laugh as a way to relieve stress is that it's safe, non-invasive and tested to be efficient. Studies have proven that laughter can be used to lower the levels of cortisol (stress hormone) and increase the endorphin (happy hormone).

Move your body. Get up from bed, step out of your chair and begin to walk, stretch, or climb up stairs. Moving your body stimulates the release of natural chemicals within your brain which will give you a feeling of well-being and reduce anxiety and stress.

Make a gratitude diary - write down those things you are grateful for. thankful. It is a great practice for your brain that promotes positive thoughts to block negative thoughts. It is possible to be thankful for even the tiniest things. It can be helpful to write it down as a means to let go of stress and get feeling great.

Be mindful of the things that go in your body

Whatever is in your body may affect the symptoms of your bipolar disorder. The result could be positive or negative dependent on the substances you consume- from your diet to supplements to your prescription medication to any other substances you consume.

If you're looking to get rid of the signs of depression and mania, take a look at these suggestions:

Make a conscious effort to eat a balanced diet. It's time to give up eating fast food as they're typically junk food, and contain a lots of harmful substances. Focus on eating fresh fruits and vegetables since these foods are abundant in the essential nutrients, both macro and micro macro, which your body requires to fight bipolar symptoms.

Get high-quality nutritional supplements. If you need to supplement your diet with nutritious foods, select the natural supplements from reliable brands. Omega 3 is the type of supplement that can provide great benefits for improving your mood. However, your main sources of the nutrient must be food items like salmon, sardines as well as nuts and seeds.

If it is necessary to take a medication such as over-the counter or prescription take care to be careful and cautious. It is always recommended to talk to your doctor about your medical condition, as the chemical compounds in medicines may trigger an allergic reaction in your body. This could lead to the process of developing either depression or mania.

Avoid using alcohol, drugs and cigarettes. They contain high levels of chemicals that can cause or make your bipolar symptoms worse. These chemicals are particularly dangerous when you're taking bipolar medications. The interaction could have serious consequences and even risk your life.

Chapter 15: Factors to Consider

While the question of what causes the causes of bipolar disorder is not yet resolved, scientists have gained a deeper understanding of the mental illness through their years of research. Here are some possible causes that could be the cause of the increased highs of mania as well as the severe depressive lows.

Genetics: Studies of bipolar sufferers and their tendencies have confirmed the notion that bipolar disorder can be passed down through families. Psychologists have also suggested that bipolar disorder might be the result of specific genes or the composition of certain chromosomes among bipolar patients. In a study that examined similar twins have revealed that when one twin is suffering from bipolar disorder the other twin is at a greater chance of having the same disorder when as compared to the other family member. They also concluded that a twin who is identical to the other will be likely to suffer from bipolar disorder with a between 40 and 50 percent.

Another study from Johns Hopkins University found that 40 percent of those 47 relatives with first degree of the bipolar II sufferers also showed symptoms of bipolar II disorder.

The study that was designed to determine the connection between genetics and bipolar disorder was conducted in Stanford University. The study revealed five percent of kids that had one biological parent who had bipolar disorder also had a mental disorder such as depression as well as attention deficit hyperactivity disorder, or ADHD.

Neurotransmitters: Experts have concluded that bipolar disorder may be due to the ineffective functioning of neurotransmitters. Neurotransmitters are brain's part which transmits messages to brain which determine the state of mind of the person. To function normally there must be a balance in brain's chemicals like serotonin, noradrenaline and dopamine. If there is a break of these chemical balances bipolar mania and depression could be caused. Serotonin and noradrenaline are often connected to psychiatric illnesses such as bipolar and depression. Serotonin plays an important role in body functions , such as sleep, wakefulness sexual activity, eating habits, and cognitive processes. Therefore, the abnormalities in brain circuits that use serotonin as the brain's messenger are a factor in mood fluctuations. The imbalance in dopamine levels can be associated with schizophrenia and psychosis.

The study of the environment and lifestyle indicate that the children of bipolar parents must face difficult, stressful situations every day. For instance, being with a parent who has a tendency to experience extreme mood swings, who drink alcohol, or other drugs that are addictive as well as indiscretions with regard to financial and sexual matters, and hospitalizations. If they are not treated, bipolar parents are likely be unable to manage their emotions and might be abusive to their children, verbally or even physically. Stressors from the environment can cause bipolar disorders in those with a genetic predisposition.

Insufficient Sleep- Medical findings highlight the impact of inadequate sleep on the duration and frequency of bipolar-related episodes. Bipolar sufferers have a genetic predisposition to unbalanced sleep-wake cycles which trigger signs of depression and depression and. In a study that examined 39 bipolar patients who were 65% bipolar, they suffered from bipolar symptoms after experiencing disturbances during their night.

Signs and symptoms

Humans usually experience their number of ups and downs in certain circumstances, but when it comes to bipolar disorder, these moods are very severe. The symptoms and signs may vary from one person to the next and there may be variations in the episodes' patterns, frequency, and length. There are four types of mood changes of bipolar disorder. They include hypomania, mania depression, and a combination of any of these three episodes. Bipolar symptoms of mania include:

1. Extreme happiness or the feeling of the feeling of.

2. Extreme optimism for a long length of time.

2. Easy to stir.

3. Talking faster than the norm or normal speed.

4. Uneasy and restless.

5. The impulsive.

6. Poor judgment or impaired.

7. Too much faith and unrealistic.

8. Perform risky and bizarre behaviours like investing the money they earn in

betting, participating in indecent sexual behavior, and blame all those who critique their actions.

9. You can sleep for longer periods of time.

10. A few people suffer from delusions or hear voices.

11. Bipolar patients can also feel as if they are superhuman in manic episodes.

Hypomania is not as severe in comparison to manic episodes. People may also be lively, however they can stay in reality. Hypomania is characterized by the following symptoms:

Irritability.

The superficial beliefs about his talents.

Doesn't get enough sleep, but is active throughout the daytime.

It speaks a little quickly.

Quickly changes their mind about certain decision.

It is difficult to concentrate.

Unthinking about the potential negative consequences.

The following symptoms are common to bipolar depression.

1. An unexpected feelings of sadness or anxious for a long period of time.

2. Inability to engage in the activities typically he enjoys when he is not suffering from symptoms.

3. Removing from family and close friendships.

4. Talk slowly.

5. Sleep a lot.

6. Inability to interact with others.

7. Bipolar sufferers may feel devalued or even guilty for a variety of reasons or even no reason at all.

8. Suicide-related thoughts may arise.

A bipolar episode that is mixed disorder is characterised by the transitions between hypomania, mania and depression. Patients with mixed episodes suffer from

1. Irritability

2. Distracting and high level

3. Anxiety attacks.

4. Sleepiness problems.

5. Race-related thoughts.

6. Suicidal attempt.

It is recommended to look professional assistance as soon as you spot these symptoms within your own or another person in your family. Bipolar disorder that is not treated properly can be harmful to all aspects of your life including your professional career, social interactions and general health.

Chapter 16: My Struggle With Bipolar Disorder

Wow! I'm not sure what to do to get started. Bipolar disorder has been an extremely emotional and intense roller coaster of moods, emotions, and behaviours for me. It's a lot like the roller coaster those who are addicted to drugs go on. Then you're in the sky , and at the same time you're in such a low state that you feel you're in the burning fiery flames of Hell.

A moment you believe that you're so powerful that you're unstoppable and that nothing could hurt you, and then you think that your sole purpose on this Earth is to commit suicide.

My actions ranged from pretending to be God to contemplating suicide. I was determined to take my own life since I believed that the god as powerful as me was not capable of living in the world.

I am able to recall the deep, dark and bleak moments of sadness and despair I felt. I was convinced that life was not worth living. I believed that I was unworthy I felt hopeless, unhelpful, and felt like the fact that I "needed to" end my life. I was apathetic about myself. I was determined to commit the last and most gruesome decision to commit suicide. I wanted all the suffering to be over.

When I was at the lowest places, I would make radical changes toward the direction of upwards. I would feel overwhelmed with an exuberant energy and believed that I was capable of accomplishing anything I wanted to do. I felt strong. I felt like a god. I believed I was more than any other person on Earth. I felt so damn elated. I was in the best mood of my the world. I was beyond "happy".

When I reached the most dangerous (and most dangerous) moment in my existence, I'd slide to depression in a rapid manner. To me there was no middle. It was either God or an insignificant, pitiful thing that was not worthy of living. There was simply no alternative.

The worst part occurred when I found myself in states of mixed emotions in which I experienced extreme sadness and extreme joy simultaneously. This is when I began to believe that I was God and that my motive was to take my own life. It was a difficult and confusing time that I had to face.

I was known to engage in risky behavior that included spending excessively and engaging in relationships with people I did not knew. I would often drive at high speeds when driving, and I had several accidents with cars. I once even decided to make a solo 2,000 mile journey with just four dollars cash and a plethora of credit cards with maxed-out balances on me. To make matters worse I had no idea any of the people in the area I believed I should be goingto!

Being a person with bipolar disorder was tough. Then I realized I needed help from a professional. Then I tried to get it for a long time and they were constantly changing my medications since I was not getting any relief. I was becoming so annoyed and it's extremely difficult to manage the world when your have a broken mind. It's like a Catch-22. If you fix your mental issue, you'll be healed. But what do you do to fix your mental issue in the event that you require the help of your "mental" to correct the issue.

After years of intensive treatments and medication changes I was able to find the perfect equilibrium in my life. It was not easy. But I won't claim it was. I've failed many times. I made plenty of mistakes. But I also gained wisdom and understanding from that extremely painful experience I lived. Now, I'm making use of what I've learned to help others so that they can also be able to find peace. They will then be able to experience the full joy of life. Therefore, I have decided to share the love to you all. If I can do it, you will too my dear friend.

Conclusion

I'm hoping that this book has given you the most important information on bipolar disorder. I'm hoping that this book could aid you, whether you suffer from this disorder , or have a loved one that suffers from this disorder.

Fighting against bipolar disorder isn't an something that is easy. Therefore, you must be remain patient. If you are aware of others who would profit from reading this, please feel at ease to share this book with them.

Now that you are aware of the power of knowledge, it's your turn to create positive changes to your life. You must stand up to fight bipolar disorder. You can win this battle.